50
WAYS

Farmers Can Protect Their Groundwater

Michael C. Hirschi
F. William Simmons
Doug Peterson
Ed Giles

Made possible with funding from the Illinois Groundwater Consortium

North Central Regional Extension Publication 522

North Central Regional Extension Publications are subject to peer review and prepared as a part of the Cooperative Extension activities of the thirteen land-grant universities of the twelve North Central States, in cooperation with the Extension Service, U.S. Department of Agriculture, Washington, D.C. The following universities cooperated in making this publication available:

University of Illinois*
Ag. Publication Office
69 Mumford Hall
Urbana, IL 61801
(217)333-2007

University of Minnesota
Distribution Center
3 Coffey Hall, 1420 Eckles Ave.
St. Paul, MN 55108-6064
(612)625-8173

University of Missouri
Extension Publications
2800 McGuire
Columbia, MO 65211-0001
(314)882-2792

*Publishing university

For copies of this and other North Central Regional Extension Publications, write to: Publications Office, Cooperative Extension Service, in care of the university listed above for your state. If they do not have copies or your university is not listed above, contact the publishing university as marked with an asterisk.

Programs and activities of the Cooperative Extension Service are available to all potential clientele without regard to race, color, national origin, age, sex, religion, or disability.

In cooperation with the NCR Educational Materials Project.

Issued in furtherance of Cooperative Extension work, Acts of Congress of May 8 and June 30, 1914, in cooperation with the U.S. Department of Agriculture and Cooperative Extension Services of Illinois, Indiana, Iowa, Kansas, Michigan, Minnesota, Missouri, Nebraska, North Dakota, Ohio, South Dakota, and Wisconsin. Donald Uchtmann, Director, Cooperative Extension Service, University of Illinois at Urbana-Champaign, Urbana, IL 61801.

March 1994

Printed and distributed in cooperation with Extension Service, U.S. Department of Agriculture, Washington, D.C., and Alabama, Delaware, Florida, Georgia, Kentucky, Maine, North Carolina, Oklahoma, South Carolina, and Washington.

Library of Congress Catalog Card Number: 93-060131
ISBN 1-883097-00-2

This publication is printed with soybean ink on recycled paper.

10M—3-94—85107—NN

Produced by Information Services, Office of Agricultural Communications and Education

Project coordinators: Gary Beaumont, Doug Peterson, Michael C. Hirschi (UI Department of Agricultural Engineering), F. William Simmons (Department of Agronomy)

Technical coordinators: Michael C. Hirschi, F. William Simmons

Writers: Doug Peterson, Ed Giles, Michael C. Hirschi, F. William Simmons

Editor: Nancy Nichols

Designer: Marisa R. Meador

Proofreader: Cheryl Frank

Technical illustrator: M.R. Greenberg, freelancer

Photo credits
Page   9 Doug Martin, *Farm Journal*
     16 Wendell Smith, *Muscoda Progressive,* Wisconsin
     25 Steve Kleeman, *Flint Journal,* Michigan
     52 Bob Coyle, *Successful Farming*
     73 Courtesy of *Wallaces Farmer*
     80 Jim Barnett, Barnett Photography, Inc., Indiana
     91 University of Illinois News Bureau
     94 David Riecks, Information Services
     95 David Riecks
   103 David Riecks
   110 David Riecks
   116 Dale Guldan, Wisconsin
   142 David Riecks
   154 David Riecks
   165 Duane Johnson, *Versailles Leader-Statesman,* Missouri
   175 Doug Carroll, *Hastings Daily Tribune,* Nebraska

Technical reviewers:
The following people reviewed the text in its entirety.

University of Illinois at Urbana-Champaign
C.D. Anderson, Extension specialist, agronomy
Peter D. Bloome, Cooperative Extension Service assistant director
Michael C. Hirschi, Extension specialist, agricultural engineering
F. William Simmons, Extension specialist, soil science
L.M. Wax, USDA Agricultural Research Service agronomist

Illinois Department of Agriculture
Warren D. Goetsch, chief, Bureau of Environmental Programs

Illinois Department of Public Health
Tom Long, toxicologist

Illinois Geological Survey
Dennis P. McKenna, associate geologist

Soil Conservation Service
Wiley Scott, water quality coordinator

Illinois State Water Survey
Brian W. Kaiser, associate chemist
Loretta M. Skowron, associate professional scientist

Farmer
Floyd D. Bohlen, Vermilion County, Illinois

The following people reviewed portions of the text.

University of Illinois at Urbana-Champaign
Kathleen Brown, Extension specialist, community development
Robert G. Hoeft, Extension specialist, agronomy
M.D. McGlamery, Extension specialist, agronomy
Arthur J. Muehling, Extension specialist, agricultural engineering
David R. Pike, Extension specialist, agronomy
Gerald L. Riskowski, agricultural engineer
John C. Siemens, Extension specialist, agricultural engineering
Kevin L. Steffey, Extension specialist, entomology
Robert E. Wolf, Extension specialist, agricultural engineering

Hazardous Waste Research and Information Center
Daniel D. Kraybill, technical assistance engineer
Jack Cochran, senior organic/analytical chemist

Illinois Environmental Protection Agency
A.G. Taylor, agricultural adviser
T.C. Hornshaw, environmental protection specialist

Also, thanks to the following people who helped with certain farmer profiles and illustrations: Carroll E. Goering and Loren E. Bode, University of Illinois; Charles Fulhage, Tom Yonke, and Jerry Carpenter, University of Missouri; Richard B. Ferguson, University of Nebraska; David W. Kammel, University of Wisconsin; and Mark A. Kuechler, Illinois Department of Public Health.

Contents

For more information

Farmer profiles

Eliminating the guesswork

Lowell Heap remembers a television commercial that ran nationally a few years back. The commercial showed a farmer pouring herbicide into a tank, and it was obvious that the farmer was just guessing on the amount.

"The ad disturbed a lot of farmers before it was finally pulled," says Heap, who farms 3,000 acres near Dewey, Illinois. "You just don't guess."

Guessing on something like pesticide and fertilizer use doesn't make sense from either an economic or an environmental perspective. Farmers know that it takes thought, planning, and careful experimentation to make responsible decisions about chemical use. It also takes up-to-date information. That's why we have prepared this book—*50 Ways Farmers Can Protect Their Groundwater.*

The fifty suggestions in this book are voluntary practices designed to reduce the risk of groundwater contamination without cutting into yields or profitability. In fact, a large number of these practices could boost profits by helping farmers cut back on chemical inputs.

To offer one example: Iowa State University research estimated that for a 100-acre field, farmers could save up to $1,000 per year by banding herbicides instead of broadcast spraying. The research, released in 1990, assumed that farmers sprayed herbicides in a 10-inch band within a 30-inch row. The additional cultivation needed with banding would reduce the $1,000 savings somewhat, but banding still comes out as a financially attractive way to reduce pesticide use.

In addition to the potential savings with these fifty recommendations, there is the benefit of protecting groundwater. It's an issue that strikes close to home. After all, over half of the U.S. population, and nine out of every ten rural citizens, depend on groundwater for their drinking water supply. They draw water from public or private wells, rather than from surface water, such as lakes or reservoirs.

Prior to the 1970s, it was commonly assumed that the earth acted as an effective filter, screening out contaminants before they reached the groundwater supply. However, that belief has been questioned as evidence of contamination gathers.

But how much evidence is there? Is groundwater contamination really a problem? The first phase of the National Pesticide Survey, presented by the U.S. Environmental Protection Agency in 1990, provided mixed results. Although surveyors found at least one pesticide in about 10 percent of the nation's community wells and 4 percent of the domestic rural wells, most of the pesticides were detected at low levels. Only 0.8 percent of the wells contained pesticides that exceeded health standards.

Nitrate was found in 52 percent of the wells serving urban and suburban areas and 57 percent of the rural wells. But again, only 1.2 percent of the urban wells and 2.4 percent of the rural wells contained concentrations that the U.S. EPA considers unsafe.

Although these results appear reassuring, it must be emphasized that this study provides only a *national* perspective. A limited number of wells were sampled in each state, so the results cannot be used to make statewide conclusions.

That's why many states have been conducting their own surveys, and the results are not always as positive. In Iowa, for example, a state survey in 1988 and 1989 showed that about 44.6 percent of the rural, private wells were contaminated with coliform bacteria. Also, about 17.9 percent of the rural population in Iowa was consuming drinking water from private, rural wells that contained unacceptably high concentrations of nitrate.

An Illinois study, released in 1992, found that an estimated 10 percent of the rural, private wells in the state, or 37,800 of them, have nitrate-nitrogen concentrations above the federal drinking water standard.

In Wisconsin, the state sampled 2,187 rural wells in 1990-91 and found triazines in 351 of them—or 16 percent. What's more, the detections in 220 of the wells were at or above the state's Preventive Action Limit (PAL) for atrazine. The PAL is not a legally enforceable standard, but it alerts Wisconsin homeowners to a potential problem.

Keep in mind, though, it's not what goes on nationally or even statewide that tells you the condition of your groundwater. Decisions must be made farm by farm and sometimes even field by field. As you will see in this book, much depends on the site conditions of your land. To assume that your water is clean or contaminated on the basis of national or state studies would just be guessing.

And as Lowell Heap noted, "You just don't guess."

Percentages of people relying on groundwater for domestic use in the United States

	Percent
Arizona, Florida, Hawaii, Mississippi, Nebraska, Nevada, New Mexico	More than 90
South Dakota	80 to 89
Delaware, Iowa, Maine	70 to 79
Alaska, Indiana, Kansas, South Carolina, Washington, Wisconsin, Utah	60 to 69
Arkansas, California, Illinois, Louisiana, Michigan, Montana, New Hampshire, North Dakota, Tennessee, Texas, Vermont, West Virginia, Wyoming	50 to 59
Georgia, Minnesota, New Jersey, New York, Ohio, Pennsylvania, Virginia	40 to 49
Alabama, Connecticut, Maryland, Massachusetts, Missouri, North Carolina, Oklahoma, Oregon	30 to 39
Colorado, Kentucky, Rhode Island	20 to 29
Puerto Rico, Virgin Islands	Less than 20

NOTE: These are the percentages of people who receive their water from either public or private wells, which draw on groundwater.

SOURCES: *Agriculture and the Environment: The 1991 Yearbook of Agriculture,* U.S. Department of Agriculture; Maryland Department of the Environment.

Nitrogen

1 Set realistic yield goals

The price of overoptimism

In farming, it can be expensive to be overoptimistic, especially when it comes to nitrogen (N) application.

Because soil tests for nitrogen are not entirely reliable, N application recommendations are based on yield goals. But if your yield goals are overly optimistic, the recommended application rates for N will be high. The result: increased expense, increased levels of N in the soil, and increased risk to groundwater.

Some studies show that farmers *do* tend to be overoptimistic about yield goals. According to a four-year survey of 158 farmers in Nebraska, only 10 percent reached their yield goal. About half of the farmers reached 80 percent of their yield goal, whereas another 40 percent of them fell more than 20 percent below their goal.

Guidelines for setting realistic yield goals

- Recognize that exceptionally good years are the exception.
- Establish realistic yield estimates for each field based on soil type, your own three- to five-year yield records, county average yields, and yields on neighboring farms. Try to ignore short-term weather conditions.
- Set your yield goal 5 to 10 percent above your average yield of the past five years. That way, if it's a good year, the crop will have enough nutrients to become a bumper crop. If it's an off year, the amount of excess nitrogen in the soil will be kept to a minimum.

2 Test the soil

The link to groundwater

Of soil nutrients, nitrogen clearly poses the most risk to groundwater. This is true whether the source of N is commercial fertilizers, animal manures, forage legumes, sewage sludge, or other forms of organic wastes.

Phosphorus (P), potassium (K), and other nutrients do *not* pose a risk to groundwater, but they still have an indirect link to groundwater quality. Nutrients often interact with one another, so a deficiency of one nutrient could mean that the plant will not effectively use another one.

To put it another way, the level of P and K can affect the plant's uptake of N, which *does* have a bearing on groundwater. The best way to ensure proper levels of P and K is with soil testing.

The link to yields

Beyond the water quality issue, there is also the obvious yield benefit of testing for all nutrients. The following University of Illinois data illustrate how adequate nutrient levels increase corn yields:

Nutrient levels and corn yields			
N	P	K	Yield
———— pounds/acre ————			bushels/acre
180	60	0	96
180	0	90	111
180	60	90	143

Soil testing helps you maintain the balance—applying enough fertilizer to maintain productivity without applying so much that it becomes uneconomical or environmentally hazardous.

Testing for N

The technology to test soil for N has its problems. But in recent years, nitrate tests have had some success in the drier, western part of the Corn Belt. Although the eastern part of the Corn Belt has had less success, improvements are being made in testing for N.

To increase the validity of N soil tests, follow two important guidelines:

- Collect samples at the depth where the plants' roots take in nutrients and moisture—anywhere from 1 to 3 feet deep. Follow sampling guidelines for the test that the lab is running.

- Test the soil for nitrogen close to the time of peak demand by the plant. If you test too early, you will not have a good idea of nitrogen content at the most crucial time of need for the plant. Nitrogen changes forms easily. So if you test too early, it may change forms and be lost through leaching or denitrification, throwing off your test results.

Testing for P and K

In contrast to testing for N, soil tests for P and K are well established and quite useful for determining phosphorus and potassium needs.

The most useful test for phosphorus is the P-1 test, which estimates the amount of P in the soil that is available to the plant. The most frequently used and best-calibrated test for K is ammonium acetate exchangeable K.

Testing for pH

Fluctuations in soil acidity can affect the availability of nutrients to plants, not to mention the levels of toxic metals in the soil and the amount of microorganism activity.

Phosphate, in particular, reacts to soil pH and is more available to the plant in slightly acidic to neutral soils. If the soil is too acidic (pH below 5.5) or too alkaline (pH above 7.3), much of the phosphate is converted to a form that is unavailable to the plant.

Researchers have found that the most effective use of nutrients occurs in corn and soybeans when the pH level is 6.0 to 7.0.

Soil testing with grids

In Ohio, the Sollars' system is producing some down-to-earth results. Mike Sollars farms 3,000 acres near the town of Washington Courthouse, and his system of soil testing is paying off.

"Right now, the cost of testing our soil is so insignificant compared to the knowledge we're getting of what our fields need," says Sollars, who farms with his three brothers and their families. It costs him less than $2 to test an acre.

Sollars used to divide his farm into 10- to 20-acre grids and then test for nutrient levels in each grid square. But after finding so much variance, he now tests in grids that cover less than 3 acres. Sollars divides the fields into 360-foot-wide grid squares that can accommodate a 40-foot fan spreader or the 60-foot boom of an air-flow spreader.

He takes a few days every year to test one-third of the acres for phosphorus, potassium, pH, lime, organic matter, magnesium, manganese, calcium, boron, and zinc. He says testing for nitrogen would be inaccurate because he tests the soil in February or March—long before the time of peak demand by the plant.

After Sollars receives the test results, he gives them to his sister-in-law, Bridget Sollars, who enters the data into a spreadsheet program. The program calculates application amounts grid by grid for a three-year nutrient buildup program.

Next, different ranges of application amounts are assigned different colors. Then the field map grids are colored accordingly for easy, in-the-field reference.

"Even if somebody didn't want to do anything about their nutrient levels, it gives you a much better idea of what's out there," Sollars says.

But Sollars has more than an inventory in mind. He has three major reasons for mapping nutrients:

1. He wants a better balance of phosphorus and potassium levels in the fields by applying more where it is needed and less where it isn't. "It makes both economic and environmental sense," Sollars says.

2. He wants more accurate lime applications to improve the effectiveness of pH-sensitive herbicides.

3. He wants to place manure where it is most needed and keep better track of exactly where it is applied.

Even though Sollars tests 3-acre grids, he figures out specific application rates for 20- to 30-acre areas because it would be impractical to tailor rates to smaller areas with the air-flow spreader. Sollars says he hopes someday to avoid this limitation by obtaining a spreader that can change nutrient rates and blends on the go.

But he warns other farmers that if they want to start testing, they have to get organized.

"You have to be organized just to speed up the sampling process," he says. "If you're not organized, it's going to take too much time, and you'll get frustrated and quit."

3 Credit other nitrogen sources

Learning the hard way

In the Big Spring Basin of northeast Iowa, farmers found that over-applying nitrogen is costly to both their pocketbooks and their environment.

Overfertilization cost the farmers $12 per acre and was pinpointed as the probable source of excessive nitrate levels in their groundwater. That area of Iowa has highly productive silt loam soils situated above fractured bedrock. The fractured bedrock provided easy routes for nutrients to enter groundwater.

Specialists in the area also came up with a major reason why nitrogen was being overapplied. When determining their application rates, farmers neglected to credit the N from other sources—previous legume crops and manure.

Adjusting the rates

When most soil-test laboratories recommend N application rates, they usually base recommendations on the crop yield goal. It's up to you to adjust these recommendations to account for N supplied by legumes, manure, other organic wastes, or residual soil nitrate.

Also, you should take into consideration the productivity of the previous year. Following drought years, it is common for sufficient N to carry over to supply part of the crop needs for the following year.

Adjusting for legumes

To take into consideration the amount of nitrogen supplied by legume crops during the previous year, use the following table. The table shows how many pounds of nitrogen per acre can be reduced from your application rate.

Recommendations for adjusting nitrogen: Legumes					
Crop to be grown	After soybeans	First year after alfalfa or clover		Second year after alfalfa or clover	
		Plants per square feet		Plants per square feet	
		5	2 to 4	Fewer than 2	5	Fewer than 5
		nitrogen reduction, pounds per acre				
Corn	40	100	50	0	30	0
Wheat	10	30	10	0	0	0

Adjusting for manure

The best way to gauge the nutrient content of manure is to have samples chemically analyzed. A laboratory analysis will tailor information to your specific farm. If you don't have manure samples analyzed, use the following guidelines to credit nitrogen and other nutrients in manure.

Recommendations for adjusting nutrients: Manure

Dry manure

Pounds of nutrients per ton of manure

	Nitrogen* (N)	Phosphorus (P)	Potassium (K)
Dairy cattle	11	5	11
Beef cattle	14	9	11
Hogs	10	7	8
Chickens	20	16	8

*When dry manure is incorporated during or immediately after it is applied, these numbers used for nitrogen credit should be cut in half. That's because about 50 percent of the total nitrogen in the manure will be available for the crop during the year following its application.

Liquid manure

Pounds of nutrients per 1,000 gallons

	Nitrogen* (N)	Phosphorus (P)	Potassium (K)
Dairy cattle	26	11	23
Beef cattle	21	7	18
Hogs	56	30	22
Chickens	74	68	27

*When liquid manure is incorporated during or immediately after it is applied, these numbers used for nitrogen credit should be cut by either 50 percent or 40 percent. That's because about 50 to 60 percent of the total nitrogen in the manure will be available to the crop during the year following its application.

4 Apply nitrogen in the spring

Fall versus spring

Your best bet is to apply nitrogen as close as possible to when your crop needs it most.

When you apply nitrogen in the fall, a portion of the N may be lost before the next spring. This loss could reduce yields, and it could mean that nitrogen will leach through the root zone, ending up in groundwater.

In fact, researchers estimate that with fall application, nitrogen losses can range from 10 to 20 percent on fine- and medium-textured soils, and 20 to 50 percent on coarse-textured soils. University of Illinois research has also shown that it can take 120 pounds of fall-applied nitrogen to produce the same yield increase as 100 pounds applied in the spring.

Because of nitrogen losses, it is especially important to avoid fall applications of nitrogen on coarse-textured soils or shallow soils over fractured bedrock. These soil conditions offer the greatest probability of leaching.

If fall applications must be made on other types of soil, only use ammonium forms of nitrogen such as anhydrous ammonia, urea, or ammonium sulfate. In addition, wait until the ground temperature has decreased to 50°F—or 60°F if you use nitrification inhibitors with anhydrous ammonia. At these temperatures, soil organisms are less active and less likely to convert ammonium to nitrate.

Of the spring applications, here are three options:

Side-dressing

Side-dressing nitrogen is probably the most effective way to increase N uptake on all soils. With side-dressing, you apply nitrogen right before the peak demand of the plant. The plant absorbs N before it has much time to leach or denitrify.

Timing is crucial because the period in which corn takes up nitrogen most rapidly is from about three to twelve weeks after planting. If you side-dress too late or if you side-dress N on dry soil that remains dry, the benefits are greatly reduced. If the weather is too wet, you may have trouble getting application equipment on the field in time.

Also, some studies have shown that there is no yield loss if you inject nitrogen in *every other* row instead of every row. With every-other-row application, each row still has nitrogen injected on one side or the other. While this does not reduce your nitrogen inputs, it does reduce the energy requirements of side-dressing.

Preplant

Preplant nitrogen applications usually will not be as effective as delayed applications—such as side-dressing on coarse-textured soils. However, on medium-textured, well-drained soils, preplant applications can be equally effective.

If you make preplant applications on sandy or poorly drained soils, apply ammonium forms and use nitrification inhibitors. This method reduces the potential for nitrogen loss through denitrification or leaching.

Split or multiple

With split or multiple applications, the application of N fertilizer is broken down into several stages. This strategy is sometimes the best way to prevent N losses on sandy soils.

Multiple applications supply N when it is most needed by the plants and allow you to adjust the timing of applications according to early season weather and soil tests.

On the other hand, multiple applications can consume more time and energy. Also, if the weather is not on your side, you may not be able to apply N at the proper time, and the result could be a nutrient deficiency.

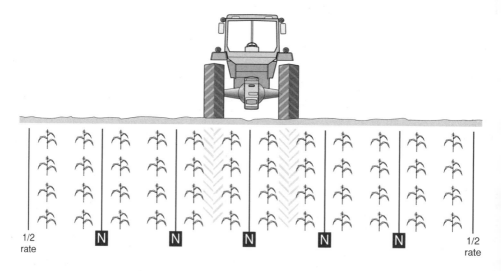

*Some studies have shown that there is no yield loss if you side-dress nitrogen in **every other** row instead of every row. In this illustration of every-other-row, side-dress injection, note that the outside two injectors are set at one-half rate. That's because the outside injectors will run between those two rows twice.*

NITROGEN FLOW METERS INCREASE EFFICIENCY

Equipment is currently available that monitors the flow rate of anhydrous ammonia and liquid nitrogen fertilizers. This equipment makes application rates more accurate by adjusting the flow rate for specific field situations as the applicator travels across the field. The equipment will even adjust the flow rate to correct for differences in tractor speed.

Side-dressing and crediting nitrogen

Robert Studnicka's nitrogen is doing a disappearing act, but he knows right where it is going.

"We have been using anhydrous ammonia, putting it on with a chisel plow and adding a nitrification inhibitor," says Studnicka. "But when we do testing a week later, we find that most of the nitrogen we put down is gone.

"It's going right into our groundwater," he says. "The water table here is 10 feet below the soil surface, which is mostly sand."

With his three brothers, Studnicka farms 2,086 acres of land (638 acres in crops) near Muscoda, Wisconsin. He says he is exploring ways to protect his groundwater with help from the University of Wisconsin's Nutrient and Pest Management Program.

"We're starting to side-dress the nitrogen, because we can get by using less nitrogen and about half-rates on the nitrification inhibitor," he says. "The inhibitor may be a good product, but when you look at the cost, it's good to be able to cut down."

Studnicka says he and his brothers are also crediting other nutrient sources that they apply to their 450 acres of corn. They broadcast 3,000 gallons per acre of liquid dairy manure—which has boosted phosphate and potash levels—and credit some of it for nitrogen. They also credit whey permeate, a nitrogen-rich dairy by-product.

"You really care about your groundwater when it's you and your family drinking it, and you have nitrate levels of 15 to 20 parts per million," Studnicka says.

5 Use nitrification inhibitors when effective

Nitrate forms

Plants can use both the ammonium and nitrate forms of nitrogen. But the nitrate form is more susceptible to leaching. It poses more risk to groundwater.

Nitrification is a process in which bacteria convert ammonium forms of nitrogen into nitrate forms. Nitrification inhibitors, therefore, are chemicals designed to slow down this process, reducing the risk of leaching and denitrification (see illustration on page 18).

When inhibitors were properly applied in one Illinois experiment, as much as 42 percent of the soil-applied ammonia remained in the ammonium form through the early part of the growing season. Without inhibitors, only 4 percent remained in the ammonium form.

However, inhibitors are not useful in all situations.

Effective uses

Certain conditions lend themselves to the use of nitrification inhibitors.

- Inhibitors should slow the processes in which N is lost if the soil is moderately or well-drained and is in an area of heavy rainfall or frequent flooding.

- When you apply nitrogen in the fall, ammonium forms of N have more time to convert into nitrate forms. As a result, there is more risk of leaching or denitrification. With the use of inhibitors, you can reduce these problems. Most of the nitrogen may remain in its ammonium form throughout the winter.

- If you plan to apply nitrogen with inhibitors in the fall, it works best to make applications after the soil temperature has dropped below 60°F and the soil is likely to be frozen for most of the winter.

- Inhibitors work best when nitrogen is applied at or below optimum levels.

- Inhibitors should *not* be viewed as a way to reduce the amount of nitrogen applied to a field, but rather as a tool for reducing N loss.

Not-so-effective uses

There are several conditions, however, in which inhibitors will not help prevent leaching.

- Inhibitors are not necessary if the nitrogen is applied right before the crop needs it. Nitrogen without inhibitors would work just as well in this case.

- Inhibitors do not work as well in extremely coarse soils. In these soils, the ammonium nitrogen has a tendency to move away from the inhibitors. However, inhibitors can be effective in coarse soils when nitrogen applications are managed carefully.

- Fall-applied inhibitors are not effective if the soil remains unfrozen for most of the winter. In such cases, bacterial processes will eventually nitrify the N. By the time spring comes, the nitrogen will be in nitrate form and will leach through the soil during spring rains or be lost through denitrification.

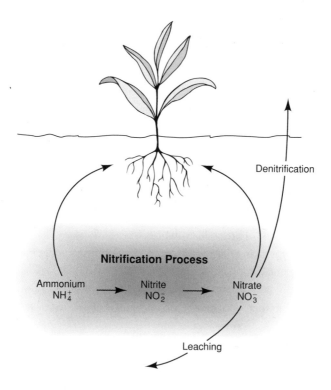

A high percentage of the nitrogen applied in the Midwest is in the ammonium form or else converts to ammonium soon after application. During the nitrification process, ammonium nitrogen changes to nitrite, which then converts to nitrate. In the nitrate form, nitrogen can be lost by denitrification or by leaching. Nitrification inhibitors slow the conversion of ammonium to nitrite.

Scouting

6 Scout fields

Integrated pest management

Scouting fields is one of the most important elements in an integrated pest management (IPM) program. Accurate and timely scouting helps you identify problems before they get out of control, and it helps you avoid battling problems that don't exist. It allows you to plan an effective pest-control program using only the management tools *essential* for control.

But before you head into the fields with a keen eye and a clipboard, ask yourself a few questions:

- Do I have time to scout?
- Do I know how and when to scout?
- Can I identify both insect pests and beneficial insects?
- Can I adequately measure insect populations and crop damage?
- Can I identify weeds when they are small enough to control?
- Can I identify weeds late in the season, so I can plan next year's control program?
- Can I identify crop diseases?
- Do I know and understand economic thresholds?
- Can I prepare a thorough set of crop scouting records?

If you answered "no" to most of these questions but still want to start a crop scouting program, contact your local Cooperative Extension Service office. The Extension Service offers field scouting and IPM education programs.

Another option is to hire an outside firm to scout your fields for you. Many private consulting firms, farmer cooperatives, pesticide dealers, and seed companies offer scouting services.

Scouting procedures

When entering a field to scout, follow these basic procedures:

1. Make sure you have the proper equipment.
2. Identify the field on a scouting report form by the field number, location, or other characteristics.
3. Record the date, time of day, and weather conditions.
4. Record the stage of growth of the crop.
5. Record general soil and crop conditions.

6. Sample the field in the pattern prescribed for the particular problem (see illustrations of patterns 1 through 3 on page 22).

7. Record the results.

Scouting patterns

As a general rule, you should enter the field about 50 paces beyond the end rows before making counts. Avoid border rows unless you are scouting for a specific type of insect that may attack these areas first.

There are three basic patterns for pest infestations in a field. That's why there are also three basic patterns for scouting (see illustrations). Keep in mind that it may be necessary to combine two or more patterns.

Additional tips

- Visit each field at least once a week. Some fields will need less frequent scouting, some will need more. Also, certain insect problems, such as black cutworms, require frequent scouting in the spring.

- When pests are *not* mobile, such as cutworms or diseases, sample plants that are next to each other.

- When pests *are* mobile, such as corn rootworm adults, sample plants that are some distance apart from one another.

- Fields planted to different crops should be sampled separately, no matter how small the field.

- If there are different hybrids in the same field, sample them separately.

- If you notice a problem but cannot determine the cause, collect a sample of the soil, plant material, or both and send it to a local or state laboratory. For example, you can send samples of weeds or injured crops (but not soil samples) to the University of Illinois Plant Clinic. For details on how to use the Plant Clinic's services, see the section "For More Information," on page 189.

- Remember to observe the proper reentry times for fields that have been treated with pesticides. If you smell an unusual odor or begin to feel strange, get out of the field.

A scouting manual

A comprehensive guide to scouting, the *Field Crop Scouting Manual*, is available from the University of Illinois. For details on how to obtain a copy, see the "For More Information" section on page 188.

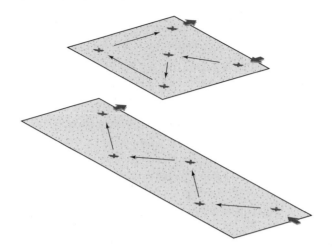

Pattern 1. *If you expect to find pests uniformly across a field, select sampling sites that are also evenly distributed. In a square field, sample the center and the four corners. In a rectangular field, you might want to make a zigzag pattern.*

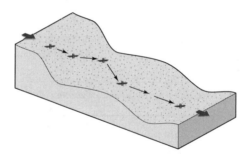

Pattern 2. *If pests tend to concentrate in particular areas, such as high or low spots, examine those spots more carefully than other areas. That way, you can determine the extent and severity of damage.*

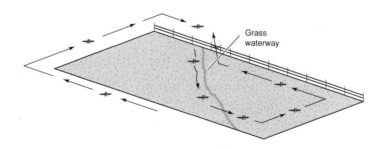

Grass
waterway

Pattern 3. *If pests first invade a field at the borders (as stalkborers and grasshoppers often do), scout along the fence lines and along any waterways that run into the field.*

SCOUTING EQUIPMENT

Be prepared

The following items can help you collect data quickly and accurately. The well-prepared field scout should have access to these tools at all times.

Sampling equipment

Beat cloth   For sampling insects in soybeans. It is placed on the ground between two rows, then plants are shaken over the cloth to dislodge insects so they can be counted.

Pocketknife   For digging out small areas of soil around plants, for splitting plants (cornstalks, alfalfa crowns) to look for insects, or for digging up weeds or injured plants.

Shovel or trowel   For sampling soil-inhabiting insects, usually in corn. It can be used early in the season to look for seedcorn maggots, white grubs, and wireworms. Later in the season, it can be used to look for corn rootworm larvae and to dig up corn plants so that roots can be examined for rootworm larval damage.

Sweep net   For sampling insects in alfalfa and drilled soybeans. Insects are collected in the sweep net and then counted.

Collecting equipment

Film canisters
Vials
Pill boxes   For collecting small insects that need to be brought back and identified.

Plastic bags
Paper bags
Wide-mouth jars   For collecting large insects. Paper and plastic bags are also used for collecting plant samples, such as damaged plants.

Isopropyl alcohol   For preserving insect specimens for later identification. This easily obtained type of alcohol can be placed in vials.

Sampling aids

County maps	For locating fields.
Forceps *Tweezers*	For picking up and manipulating small insects, or for teasing apart small areas on a plant.
Hand counter	For counting insects and plants. Without one, you run the risk of losing your count.
10X magnifying *glass*	For identifying small insects and weeds or examining plant parts for insects and diseases.
50-foot *measuring tape*	For taking samples in a designated length—every foot of row or every 1/1,000 of an acre, for instance. It is also used when determining plant populations.

Identification materials

Books *Picture sheets*	For accurate identification of a pest or crop injury.

Recording equipment

Clipboard	For easy writing.
Pencils *Survey forms*	For obvious use. Blank paper can be used as survey forms, but forms prepared ahead of time are usually more efficient.

Miscellaneous

First-aid kit	For obvious use. Be sure to include salt tablets for hot weather.

Scouting for big savings

Hiring someone to scout your fields may be the best money you'll ever spend, especially if you're in continuous corn, says Michigan farmer Bill Hunt.

"You'll get a good return on your money," he notes.

Actually, in Hunt's case, "good return" is an understatement. As the result of scouting, he estimates that he doesn't apply insecticides on 800 to 1,000 of his acres—acres he would have routinely treated.

Assuming that insecticide treatments cost about $10 per acre, that means he saves from $8,000 to $10,000 per year. The scouting program, on the other hand, costs him about $1,000 to $2,000 per year, so the savings is still substantial.

Hunt contracts with a company that will scout insects for a per-acre rate or a per-hour rate. He finds that the per-hour rate comes out cheaper, although an hourly fee could build up if serious problems were encountered.

Hunt grows about 4,300 to 4,400 acres of corn, depending on the year, and about 2,500 to 3,000 acres of it is continuous corn.

On the acreage where insecticide treatment is still necessary, Hunt finds other ways to cut costs. In 1990, he participated in a Michigan State University test project, in which he applied three-quarter rates. The results were so successful, Hunt continued to apply three-quarter rates on his own in 1991. He now hopes to try one-half rates on some test strips.

"I question the recommended rates of many insecticides," Hunt says.

However, he stresses that a lot depends on the climate. In Michigan, he says, pressure from corn borers and rootworms is not as great as in warmer areas of the Midwest.

If you consider hiring someone to scout your fields, Hunt says it is important to get professionals. When he and some other farmers tried hiring nonprofessionals one year, the results were not good.

As he puts it, "If you don't trust the people doing the scouting, you're just wasting your money."

Insecticides

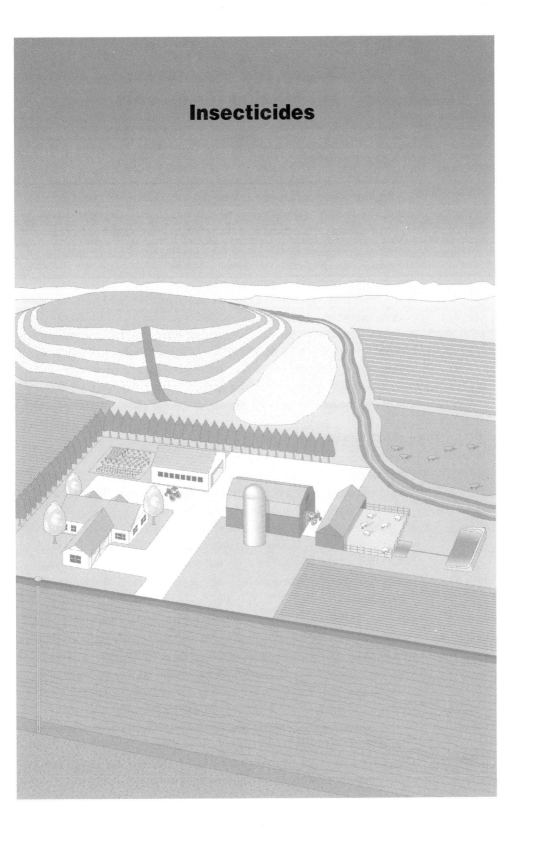

7 Know the economic thresholds for insects

What are thresholds?

When a specific insect population in your field reaches a certain level, controlling the insect to prevent it from causing economic loss is justified. This level is called the economic threshold, or the action threshold.

The economic threshold is always slightly less than the economic injury level (EIL)—the level at which a pest population is sufficiently high to cause significant crop damage. The EIL often means that the cost of crop damage by a pest *equals* the cost to control the pest population.

When a pest population reaches the economic threshold, you can take action to control it before it reaches the EIL.

Specific economic thresholds have been developed for each type of insect. Sometimes, these thresholds are expressed as numbers of insects—the average number of bean leaf beetles per foot of row, for instance. Other times, economic thresholds are expressed as a level of damage—the percentage of soybean pods injured within a field.

Imperfect tools

Keep in mind, however, that economic thresholds are guides, not gospel. They can help you determine when insecticide applications are economically warranted, and they can help you avoid making needless applications. But thresholds are far from perfect.

Most currently used thresholds are rather simplistic. They do not take into consideration what happens when there are multiple pests in a field. Also, they can be affected by many economic and environmental factors:

Crop value. As the price paid for a crop increases, the economic threshold decreases.

Cost of control. As the cost of control increases, the economic threshold increases.

Crop stress. As stress on a crop increases, the economic threshold may decrease. For instance, if a crop is already under stress from weeds, disease, lack of moisture, or lack of fertility, insect control may be economically justified even if the insect population is below the threshold.

Although many economic thresholds available today do not take these factors into consideration, a growing number of them do. A case in point: Many states have developed excellent, comprehensive worksheets that help you determine economic thresholds for European corn borers. To obtain copies of these worksheets, contact your nearest Cooperative Extension Service office.

If a comprehensive threshold hasn't been developed for a particular pest, don't be discouraged from using the available threshold. Despite limitations of less-comprehensive thresholds, they are helpful guides.

Know your pests

To make use of economic thresholds, it helps to understand how the populations of different insects change over time. It helps to know an insect's feeding habits and the conditions under which it thrives. And it helps to know whether an insect is an occasional or perennial pest.

Occasional pests. These pests usually do not cause economic damage during average years. It takes certain environmental conditions to boost their population above average and pose a threat. For example, the normal population of spider mites usually does not pose a threat to soybeans. But if weather is hot and dry, spider mite numbers go up and economic damage can result.

Perennial pests. These pests tend to cause damage almost every year, so they must be carefully monitored and controlled.

New directions

You may also want to monitor the progress of new research that could incorporate environmental concerns into economic thresholds. Researchers at Iowa State University and the University of Nebraska recently asked thousands of farmers how much they were willing to spend per acre to protect their groundwater, wildlife, beneficial insects, and other natural resources from insecticide contamination.

Using the farmers' responses, the researchers calculated "environmental costs" for 32 common insecticides. If you add these costs into the economic threshold equation, you will have to accept more crop loss before you begin chemical control of the pests. But in the long run, you could be protecting your groundwater and other resources.

Putting the environment into economic thresholds is still a new idea, but years ago the economic thresholds that are popular today seemed just as far off on the horizon.

Threshold information

For detailed information on thresholds for particular crop pests, see the *Field Crop Scouting Manual*, available from the University of Illinois. To find out how to order the manual, check the "For More Information" section on page 188.

Also, you can obtain more information on thresholds by contacting your nearest Extension office.

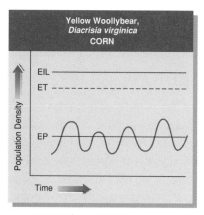

Yellow Woollybear,
Diacrisia virginica
CORN

Nonpests. *The average population density, or equilibrium position (EP), of nonpests is well below the economic threshold. These pests never reach a population level high enough to cause an economic loss.*

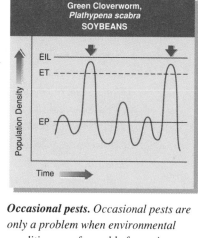

Green Cloverworm,
Plathypena scabra
SOYBEANS

Occasional pests. *Occasional pests are only a problem when environmental conditions are favorable for an increase in population. That's when population levels exceed the economic threshold. Most agricultural pests are occasional pests.*

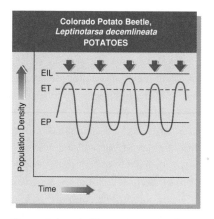

Colorado Potato Beetle,
Leptinotarsa decemlineata
POTATOES

Perennial pests. *The average population density of perennial pests is only slightly below the economic injury level. As a result, perennial pests exceed the economic threshold regularly. Agricultural pests that fall into this category require a carefully designed integrated pest management program.*

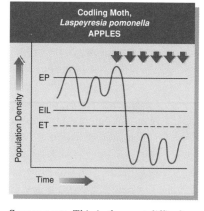

Codling Moth,
Laspeyresia pomonella
APPLES

Severe pests. *This is the most difficult category of pests to manage. For these pests, the average population density is **above** the economic injury level. Routine pesticide applications are often necessary to produce marketable crops.*

EP   Equilibrium position (the average population density)
ET   The economic threshold
EIL The economic injury level
⬇ Arrows pointing down show when insecticide was applied

8 Consider insect-resistant crop varieties

Thorns and tough roots

Plants have many natural mechanisms to keep insects at bay: repellent or toxic chemicals, thorns, hairs, and tough roots and stems.

Seed companies try to tap into these mechanisms by developing crop varieties that are resistant to certain insects and diseases, while still producing a good yield. But like everything else, there are both pros and cons to resistant varieties.

The pros

- Resistant crop varieties will not interfere with other pest-management techniques such as crop rotation or insecticide application.
- They are usually the same price or only a bit more expensive than other seeds.
- They may reduce the need for certain insecticide treatments, reducing costs and protecting groundwater.

The cons

- Resistant varieties are usually only resistant to one or a limited number of pests.
- When resistant crops are being developed, some positive traits (such as high yield) may be inadvertently lost while other traits are strengthened.
- Some resistant varieties spend more of their resources protecting themselves; subsequently, their yields may drop.
- If resistant varieties are widespread and insect populations are high, insects will develop new strains that are not affected by the plant's defenses.

The following is a chart of some pests that are affected by resistant crops. To do further research, contact your seed dealer and other farmers in the area.

Corn

European corn borer

- Screening trials conducted by seed companies since the 1960s have selected varieties less susceptible to infestation, stalk breakage, and yield reduction. But factors that increase resistance have not always been identified.

- In some varieties, high levels of the plant chemical DIMBOA in young corn plants will kill first-generation corn borers. Other unidentified factors reduce tunneling by second-generation borers.

- Researchers at the University of Missouri found that 90 percent of the hybrids produced by the seed industry have some resistance to whorl leaf feeding, and 75 percent have some resistance to sheath and collar feeding.

Corn rootworms

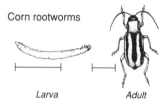

Larva   *Adult*

- Varieties with larger root masses and greater regrowth of roots may show greater "standability" or reduced lodging.

- Data on varietal differences in rooting habits or rootworm resistance are not available.

Soybeans

Potato leafhopper

- The hairiness of stems, leaves, and pods deters feeding by potato leafhoppers.

Spider mites

Actual size: the size of a period

- In variety trials conducted in 1988 (during a severe outbreak of the twospotted spider mite), the variety Burlison was the least damaged. The source of its possible resistance or tolerance has not been identified. Also, its performance under rigorous screening for resistance to spider mites has not been evaluated.

Bean leaf beetle and Mexican bean beetle

- Hairiness may deter pod-feeding beetles.
- An experimental Maturity Group III germ line, generally resistant to foliage feeders, has been identified in breeding programs at Purdue University. However, this germ line is low-yielding, and resistance factors have not yet been incorporated into agronomically acceptable commercial varieties.

⊢——————⊣ Indicates actual size of insect

Wheat

Hessian fly

Pupa ("flaxseed")
Actual size of adult: smaller than a mosquito

Pupa *Actual size of adult:*
("flaxseed") *smaller than a mosquito*

- Twenty different genes that build resistance into plants have been identified. But only five of them have been used in commercial varieties. Also, many of these resistant qualities have been overcome by new strains of the fly. Efforts to use other resistance genes in wheat varieties are ongoing.
- When a wheat variety is not effectively resistant to Hessian flies, other strategies become especially important—residue destruction, crop rotation, and strict adherence to fly-free planting dates.

Alfalfa

Aphids (spotted alfalfa, pea, and blue alfalfa aphids)

- A plant's physical characteristics, especially hairiness, interfere with aphids' ability to feed.
- Alfalfa resists the blue alfalfa aphid mainly by developing tolerance to damage.

Potato leafhopper

- Plant hairiness interferes with feeding and egg laying.
- Saponins and other plant chemicals may convey "nonpreference." Nonpreference means the insect will *not* select the plant as a source of food or as an egg-laying site. ·
- The hardening of plant stems may reduce egg laying by potato leafhoppers.

Alfalfa weevil

- Heavy terminal growth and axillary branching help the plant develop tolerance to insect damage.
- No truly resistant varieties are available.

⊢――――⊣ Indicates actual size of insect

9 Spot-treat insect infestations when possible

Distribution patterns

Some common insect pests can be controlled without treating an entire field with insecticide. Knowing the distribution patterns of the pests in your fields can help you determine whether you must spray the whole field, or just certain spots.

Stalk borers, wireworms, grasshoppers, and twospotted spider mites are pests that can often be controlled by spot treatment.

Stalk borer

Stalk borers often lay eggs during the summer in fencerows, grass conservation lanes, or grassy terraces. When corn is planted next to these areas during the following spring, there is a risk that stalk borer larvae will move from the grassy areas and infest the crop.

Ideally, you should spot-treat by applying postemergence sprays along the field edges. This prevents the larvae from moving from the weeds to the young corn plants. If you miss this chance, and if the stalk borer larvae *do* infest the small corn plants, it is usually too late to do anything except consider replanting the infested area of the field.

If you must replant, and if you cannot disk under the damaged plants, apply an insecticide as soon as the plants begin to spike. This treatment should prevent larvae from infesting the most recently planted corn.

Also, controlling weed and grass growth in and around your fields can help minimize stalk borer populations.

Wireworms

Wireworms tend to cluster in bottomlands, low spots, or other unique areas in fields. The greatest potential for wireworm infestation is in fields in which small grain or grasses have been grown for two or three years.

To determine if you should spot-treat or treat the entire field for wireworms, set simple traps two to three weeks before planting corn. Distribute traps evenly to obtain representative samples from the entire field. To find out how to set a trap, refer to the accompanying illustration.

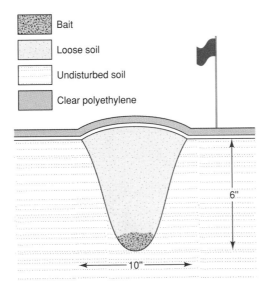

Bait

Loose soil

Undisturbed soil

Clear polyethylene

6"

10"

To determine the extent of a wireworm problem, set wireworm traps one to two weeks before planting corn. Here are the steps:

1. *Mix 1 cup wheat and 1 cup shelled corn as the bait.*

2. *Bury the bait 4 to 6 inches deep. Cover with loose soil and an 18-inch, clear plastic sheet that will collect heat and speed germination of the bait.*

3. *Mark each station with a flag or stake.*

4. *Come back in 10 to 14 days and count the number of wireworms in the traps.*

If you find one or more wireworms in each trap, you may have to treat the entire field. But if some traps are empty and others have several wireworms, you may be able to limit your treatment to the areas where you found the infested traps.

Grasshoppers

The primary grasshopper species in most of the Midwest lay eggs in late summer and fall in noncrop areas, such as roadsides, fencerows, and field edges. After the eggs hatch in spring, grasshopper nymphs feed in noncrop areas for roughly 40 to 60 days.

This is the time when grasshoppers can be managed easily by spot-treating the noncrop areas. At this stage, the grasshoppers are not very mobile and their cuticle (skin) is thin, making them easier to kill with insecticides.

These young grasshoppers will feed harmlessly in noncrop areas during the spring and early summer. But if populations reach 15 to 20 per square yard, consider spraying the noncrop areas and border rows because the grasshoppers may soon move into your fields.

If you don't get the grasshoppers early enough to prevent them from invading your field, wait until the populations in the field have passed the economic threshold before spraying. In warm, humid weather, fungal and bacterial diseases may develop among the grasshoppers, reduce their numbers, and even make chemical treatment unnecessary.

Twospotted spider mite

Spider mites complete a generation in only one to three weeks, depending on environmental conditions. This short life cycle allows spider mite populations to build up rapidly in hot, dry weather.

Spider mites usually overwinter in grassy areas in field margins. When their numbers build up during hot, dry weather, they may move from these border areas into the field edges. Therefore, spot-treating border rows and other infested areas before the spider mites move farther into a field is the best way to handle them.

Keep in mind that mite damage may not show up immediately. If you find a damaged area, you should also examine the area around the damage to determine if mites are present. If they are, spray the area surrounding the damage to make sure the infestation does not spread.

10 Know how tillage affects insects

Trade-offs

Environmental issues are rarely cut and dried. In agriculture, this is most evident when it comes to tillage.

In the 1970s, farmers nationwide shifted millions of acres into conservation tillage to protect the soil from erosion. And it paid off. The protective cover of crop residue brought erosion rates down. But there was a trade-off. Crop residue also provided a habitat for certain insects. In certain no-till situations, some farmers have experienced more insect pest problems.

Although some insects may be more of a problem in reduced-tillage and no-till fields during certain years, do not let insect concerns prevent you from adopting conservation tillage practices. Insect problems can still be controlled, and insecticide use doesn't necessarily need to increase. You can readily adapt other pest-management techniques to conservation tillage systems.

With that qualifier in mind, it's important to know how tillage might affect different insects. Below is a list of some major insect pests and the possible effects of conservation tillage on their population.

Effects of reduced tillage or no-till on insects		
Corn		
Pest	*Potential effect*	*Notes*
Armyworm	0 to ++	Ryegrass and other grass cover crops are attractive to egg-laying armyworm moths. In no-till systems where the grass cover is not plowed under, larvae move from grass to feed on corn.

NOTE: ++ = substantial increase in pest population
+ = some increase
0 = no effect
− = some decrease in pest population

⊢————⊣ Indicates actual size of insect

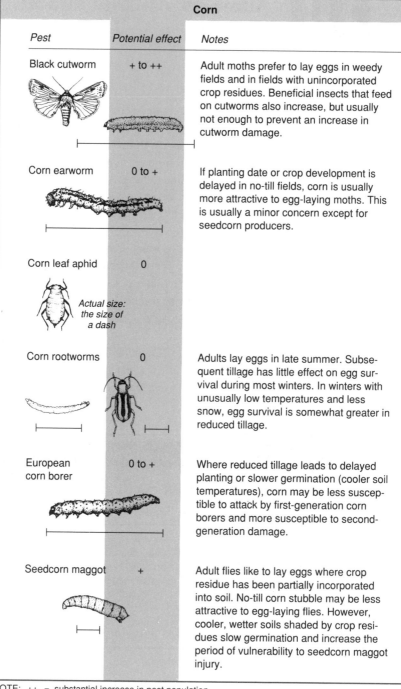

Corn

Pest	Potential effect	Notes
Black cutworm	+ to ++	Adult moths prefer to lay eggs in weedy fields and in fields with unincorporated crop residues. Beneficial insects that feed on cutworms also increase, but usually not enough to prevent an increase in cutworm damage.
Corn earworm	0 to +	If planting date or crop development is delayed in no-till fields, corn is usually more attractive to egg-laying moths. This is usually a minor concern except for seedcorn producers.
Corn leaf aphid	0	*Actual size: the size of a dash*
Corn rootworms	0	Adults lay eggs in late summer. Subsequent tillage has little effect on egg survival during most winters. In winters with unusually low temperatures and less snow, egg survival is somewhat greater in reduced tillage.
European corn borer	0 to +	Where reduced tillage leads to delayed planting or slower germination (cooler soil temperatures), corn may be less susceptible to attack by first-generation corn borers and more susceptible to second-generation damage.
Seedcorn maggot	+	Adult flies like to lay eggs where crop residue has been partially incorporated into soil. No-till corn stubble may be less attractive to egg-laying flies. However, cooler, wetter soils shaded by crop residues slow germination and increase the period of vulnerability to seedcorn maggot injury.

NOTE: ++ = substantial increase in pest population
+ = some increase
0 = no effect
− = some decrease in pest population

├────────┤ Indicates actual size of insect

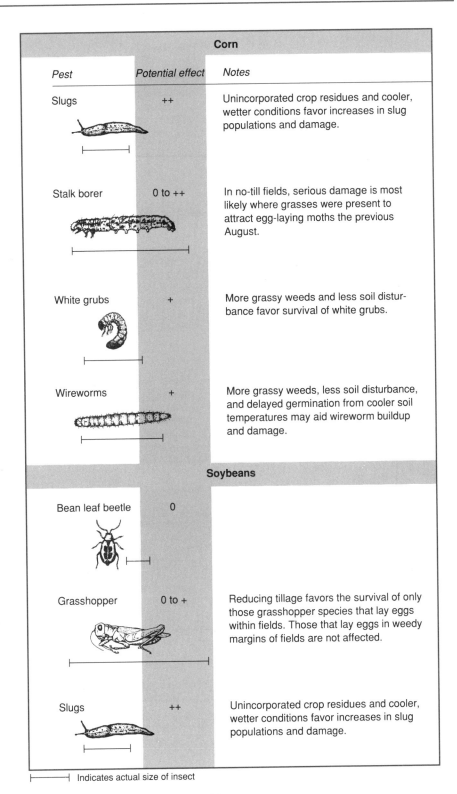

Corn

Pest	Potential effect	Notes
Slugs	++	Unincorporated crop residues and cooler, wetter conditions favor increases in slug populations and damage.
Stalk borer	0 to ++	In no-till fields, serious damage is most likely where grasses were present to attract egg-laying moths the previous August.
White grubs	+	More grassy weeds and less soil disturbance favor survival of white grubs.
Wireworms	+	More grassy weeds, less soil disturbance, and delayed germination from cooler soil temperatures may aid wireworm buildup and damage.

Soybeans

Pest	Potential effect	Notes
Bean leaf beetle	0	
Grasshopper	0 to +	Reducing tillage favors the survival of only those grasshopper species that lay eggs within fields. Those that lay eggs in weedy margins of fields are not affected.
Slugs	++	Unincorporated crop residues and cooler, wetter conditions favor increases in slug populations and damage.

├───────┤ Indicates actual size of insect

Soybeans

Pest	Potential effect	Notes
Spider mites *Actual size: the size of a period*	– to 0	Where crop residues help slow moisture loss, plants may be less drought-stressed than in conventional tillage. Reducing drought stress slows mite outbreaks.

Wheat

Pest	Potential effect	Notes
Aphids *Actual size: the size of a dash*	– to 0	Crop residues may decrease the attractiveness of new stands of wheat to airborne aphids in the fall. (Seeding wheat after Hessian fly-free dates also prevents most fall infestations of aphids.) By spring, it is unlikely that prior crop residues will affect aphid invasion.
Hessian fly *Actual size: smaller than a mosquito*	0 to ++	Hessian fly populations carry over where wheat stubble is not tilled and volunteer wheat is not controlled. Flies from undisturbed stubble move to new wheat that is planted before fly-free dates. No-till seeding of wheat into other crop residues poses no problem.

Alfalfa

Pest	Potential effect	Notes
Various pests	– to +	Several insects damage new stands of alfalfa that are no-till seeded in the fall. No-till seedings in the spring (into grasses) are less damaged than conventional seedings by potato leafhopper.

NOTE: ++ = substantial increase in pest population
   + = some increase
   0 = no effect
   − = some decrease in pest population

├───────┤ Indicates actual size of insect

Know how crop rotation affects insects

How effective are rotations?

Crop rotations do not solve all insect problems—or even most of the problems. But rotations do their best job controlling pests that are relatively nonmobile and feed on specific crops.

Of these pests, rotations most effectively control the ones that overwinter in the soil as eggs or partially grown larvae. By rotating to a different crop, you prepare a surprise for these pests when they become more active in the spring. They discover that their food source is gone.

Although crop rotations cannot solve all problems, they help manage some of the worst pests, such as northern and western corn rootworms. When you help manage some of the worst pests, you reduce insecticide use, save money, and protect groundwater.

Targeting pests

The key to crop rotation is to determine which pests you are most worried about and then rotate your crops accordingly.

In making choices, note that if a rotation cycle includes legumes, it can help build or maintain soil structure and fertility. Also, keep in mind that soybeans and alfalfa have long roots, which can take up nitrogen that may have leached past corn in a previous year. As a result, your groundwater is spared the increased nitrate risk. When the legumes are harvested, some of the nutrient remains behind to decompose back into the soil.

The following chart describes common rotation patterns and their effects on insects.

Effects of crop rotation on insects		
Rotation	Insects managed	Problem insects
Corn after corn	Wireworms and white grubs are less of a problem for two reasons: (a) They are controlled by soil insecticides used to control rootworms; and (b) adults prefer to deposit eggs in other crops.	Western and northern corn rootworms often occur at damaging levels whenever corn is planted after corn. This problem outweighs the benefits of reducing wireworms and white grubs.

Rotation	Insects managed	Problem insects
Corn after soybeans	Western and northern corn rootworms are controlled. Wireworms and white grubs usually do not build up to damaging levels in a corn-soybean rotation.	Black cutworms are slightly more common in corn after soybeans than in corn after corn. A bigger problem is that cutworm moths like to lay eggs in weedy fields in March and April. These fields are most likely to suffer cutworm damage later.
Corn after wheat	Western and northern corn rootworms are managed by any rotation that disrupts corn after corn.	Armyworms, wireworms, and white grubs may infest wheat and then cause economic damage to corn, especially in a no-till system.
Corn after alfalfa (or clover or other hay)	Western and northern corn rootworms are managed by any rotation that disrupts corn after corn.	Wireworms and cutworms are more common (but still sporadic) in corn after legumes and other perennial crops. Grape colaspis may cause economic damage to corn after red clover.
Corn after sod or set-aside	Western and northern corn rootworms are managed by any rotation that disrupts corn after corn.	Wireworms, white grubs, corn billbugs, cutworms, armyworms, and sod webworms are more common.
Continuous soybeans	None.	Grape colaspis, as well as diseases and nematodes, are more common.
Continuous wheat	None.	Hessian fly infestations may build up if fly-free dates are not observed and resistant crop varieties are not used.

12 Adjust planting and harvesting dates to control insects

Be specific

Adjusting your planting and harvesting dates can sometimes help you avoid certain insect infestations, reducing the need for chemical control. But adjusting planting and harvesting dates can backfire if you don't think it out carefully.

Planting your crop at an earlier or later date may reduce infestations of one type of pest, but it may also increase the chances of a different infestation. So adjust your crop timing only for specific crops and for specific pest problems.

You should also consider other conditions, such as soil temperature early in the season, rainfall, and tillage method. These conditions can sometimes reduce the effectiveness of your timing adjustments. Scouting your fields can help you to determine what pest problems you may have and what conditions exist in your fields.

Here are some of the effects of adjusting planting and harvesting dates, according to crop.

For corn growers...

Benefits of early planting

- Black cutworms may do less damage because the corn has grown past its vulnerable stage by the time cutworm larvae can do harm.
- Early tillage destroys weeds, where black cutworms lay most of their eggs.
- Moths that lay second-generation European corn borer eggs prefer the least mature corn, so planting early makes your corn less susceptible to the second generation.

Drawbacks of early planting

- Corn that develops early is attractive to moths that lay eggs early in the season for first-generation European corn borers.
- If you plant early, and if seed germination is delayed by cold, wet soils, there could be more damage from seedcorn beetles, seedcorn maggots, and wireworms.
- Corn rootworm larvae have a greater chance of survival.

Benefits of late planting

- Seedcorn beetles, seedcorn maggots, wireworms, and corn rootworms may do less damage to corn planted later.
- There may be a decrease in the severity of infestation by first-generation European corn borers.

Drawbacks of late planting

- There may be an increased infestation of black cutworms and second-generation European corn borers.
- Corn rootworm beetles lay more eggs in late-planted corn, and the eggs overwinter. As a result, there are more larvae to damage the crop's roots in the following summer.

For soybean growers...

Planting dates have only minor impacts on insect and mite pests of soybeans. But it still helps to note which pests are more common in early or late plantings of soybeans.

Benefits of late planting

- Overwintered, adult bean leaf beetles may cause less damage to seedlings.
- Seedcorn maggots may cause less preemergence damage.
- In cool, wet soils, there may be less preemergence damage from damping-off fungi.

Drawbacks of late planting

- Late-summer infestations of bean leaf beetles, stink bugs, and grasshoppers may cause more pod damage.

For wheat growers...

Wheat growers should adjust their planting dates to avoid infestation by the formidable, but easily avoided, Hessian fly.

Hessian fly adults lay eggs in wheat seedlings planted in the autumn. But if you wait until these adult flies have died before planting, you can seed wheat in the autumn without the risk of infestation. Destroying volunteer or set-aside wheat in the late summer is also necessary for Hessian fly control.

You can find out when it is safe to seed wheat by contacting your local Cooperative Extension Service office or a university entomologist. Depending on the climate in your region, these dates could range from mid-September to mid-October.

For alfalfa growers...

Planting dates have little effect on insect infestations in alfalfa, but harvesting dates can be important.

An early first cutting can help, as long as it does not reduce yields. It can reduce alfalfa weevil larvae infestations by exposing the larvae to sunlight, dry conditions, and more predators.

Many leafhoppers and their eggs can be removed in the second or third cuttings. But fields should then be scouted within a few days after cutting to determine the number of leafhoppers still in the field.

Insects in corn: How planting dates affect them

Pest	Early planting	Late planting
Black cutworms	Decrease	Increase
Corn rootworm larvae	Increase	Decrease*
First-generation European corn borers	Increase	Decrease
Second-generation European corn borers	Decrease	Increase
Seedcorn beetles	Increase**	Decrease
Seedcorn maggots	Increase**	Decrease
Wireworms	Increase**	Decrease

NOTE: "Decrease" means the risk of damage is decreased. "Increase" means the risk of damage is increased.

* Be aware, however, that corn rootworm beetles lay more eggs in late-planted corn. The eggs overwinter, and as a result there are more larvae to damage the crop's roots in the following summer.

** The risk only increases if seed germination is delayed by cold, wet soils.

Insects in soybeans: How late planting affects them

Pest	Late planting
Bean leaf beetles, overwintered adults feeding on seedlings	Decrease
Bean leaf beetles, late-summer infestations	Increase
Damping-off fungi	Decrease*
Grasshoppers, late-summer infestations	Increase
Seedcorn maggots	Decrease
Stink bugs, late-summer infestations	Increase

NOTE: "Decrease" means the risk of damage is decreased. "Increase" means the risk of damage is increased.

* In cool, wet soils.

13 Conserve beneficial insects

Predators and parasites

Some bugs are on your side. They are known as beneficial insects, and they fall into two main categories: predators and parasites.

Predators hunt and feed on pests. Common examples include praying mantids, lady beetles, and green lacewings.

Parasites are born inside or on a pest, and then they eat the pest as they grow. Many parasites are tiny wasps that don't sting humans but lay their eggs inside other insects.

Some companies sell predators or parasites for release in the field, but often they are expensive and ineffective. Currently there is not enough knowledge about beneficial insects to determine when to release them and how many to release.

Your best bet for now is to *conserve* the beneficial insects already in your field. Keeping these bugs alive may help to keep your pest problem at an acceptable level so you can reduce your insecticide use.

There are no easy answers for keeping beneficial insects alive, but the guidelines listed below should be a good start. Then you can find out what works best on your land.

Five steps to conserving beneficial insects

1. *Recognize the difference between pests and beneficial insects.* To decide whether you need to take control measures, you must be able to distinguish a pest from a beneficial insect. For assistance and information on identifying beneficial insects, contact the nearest Cooperative Extension Service office.

2. *Minimize insecticide applications.* Many insecticides are nonspecific, which means they kill all insects, including the ones you want to keep. Also, many beneficial insects take longer to return to treated fields than do pests.

   Therefore, try to reduce insecticide use by rotating crops, altering planting and harvesting dates, and using resistant crop varieties. Set realistic yield goals, and use economic thresholds. Then only apply insecticides if the threshold has been exceeded.

3. *Use selective insecticides and apply them selectively.* The ideal insecticide would be one that only kills the particular pest you have targeted. But most insecticides are not this selective. Nevertheless, shop carefully and you may find an insecticide that is more directly aimed at your pest problem.

If possible, use spot-treatment methods. When it is necessary to apply insecticides on an entire field, only apply when pest levels exceed the economic threshold. In addition, use the most accurate application methods whenever you can.

4. ***Maintain the habitat of beneficial insects.*** Beneficial insects are often slow to colonize a field. The best way to make sure they are nearby is to maintain their natural habitats. You can do this by leaving crop residue on the ground and preserving woodlots, windbreaks, fencerows, and unmowed grassy ditch banks and waterways.

Maintaining standing crops also improves the survival chances of beneficial insects. For instance, harvesting alternate strips of alfalfa on a schedule that allows several days of regrowth before the remaining strips are cut helps to preserve beneficial insects in alfalfa. If the entire crop is harvested at once, beneficial insects either leave the field or die.

Increasing crop diversity also increases the population of beneficial insects.

5. ***Provide pollen, nectar sources, or artificial food.*** Adults of some beneficial insects need to feed on pollen and nectar. Plants with very small flowers (such as some clovers and Queen Anne's lace) and some flowering weeds in and around the fields may help keep a diversity of insect life in your fields.

In addition, artificial food supplements that contain yeast, whey proteins, and sugars can attract or increase the numbers of adult lacewings, lady beetles, and syrphid flies.

Important considerations

Although the first three points mentioned above are excellent ideas for any field management, the last two must be thought through carefully.

Maintaining habitats and providing artificial food do more than just attract beneficial insects. These strategies can attract pests as well. So you must carefully examine your yield goals and farming methods to determine whether you can afford a wide range of insects competing in your field.

Also, keep in mind that although it is important to bring pest populations below economic thresholds, it is not necessary to *completely* eradicate pests. In fact, leaving some pests alive will help maintain the populations of beneficial insects. If you eradicate all pests, then your beneficial insects will leave in search of other food sources.

Limitations

In many cases, conserving beneficial insects will provide better natural control of insect pests. But natural control does have its limitations.

- Predators and parasites work slowly. With insecticides, farmers are used to seeing quick results. In contrast, it may take many seasons for beneficial insect populations to build up.

- When pests become few and far between, the natural enemies leave the field in search of more prey. So you are always left with a moderate number of pests still in the field.

Despite the limitations, maintaining and cultivating natural enemies is not difficult. It could save you some money on insecticides. And it could save you some trouble with your groundwater.

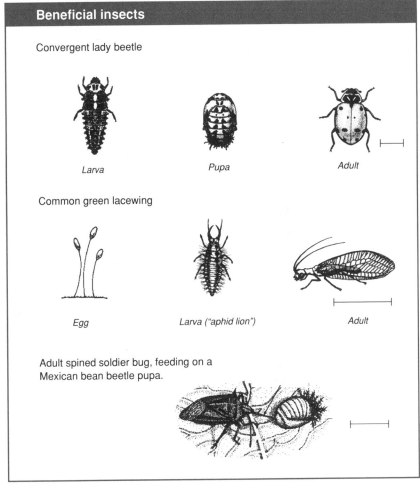

Beneficial insects

Convergent lady beetle

Larva   Pupa   Adult

Common green lacewing

Egg   Larva ("aphid lion")   Adult

Adult spined soldier bug, feeding on a Mexican bean beetle pupa.

⊢————⊣ Indicates actual size of adult insect

Chinese praying mantid

Egg case with newly
hatched nymphs

Adult
Actual size: about 3 to 4 inches

Predatory mite

adult and egg
Actual size: the size of
a period

Trichogramma wasp

Adult
Actual size: the size of a period

Big-eyed bug

Common damsel bug

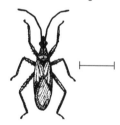

Ground beetle

Minute pirate bug

Actual size: the size of a dash

⊢——⊣ Indicates actual size of adult insect

Some important lady beetles

Seven spotted
lady beetle

Spotted lady
beetle

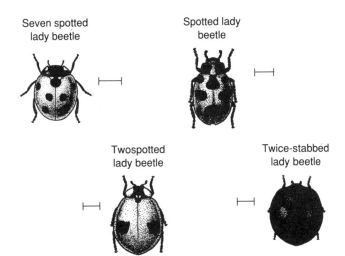

Twospotted
lady beetle

Twice-stabbed
lady beetle

Syrphid fly

Rove beetle

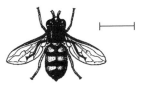

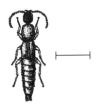

Larva

Adult

├──────┤ Indicates actual size of adult insect

Cutting rates, controlling pests, and conserving beneficials

His neighbors call him "the bug man," and if insects could talk, they would call him "sir."

Norm Larson operates a large family partnership near Maple Park, Illinois, and has gained a statewide reputation for his aggressive, innovative approach to insect control.

Since the 1990 season, Larson has been part of a University of Illinois research project comparing full rates, three-quarter rates, and one-half rates of soil insecticide. Like most farmers in the study, Larson says that cutting back to three-quarter rates was quite successful. But one-half rates didn't work as well.

"The U of I research also showed that many fields do not need insecticide treatment at all, *even* when corn follows corn," Larson says. "But the question is, 'Which fields?' That's the problem. And that's why scouting is so critical."

Larson first hired a scouting service in 1982, and since then he has developed his own program.

"It has definitely paid off," he says. "It costs about $12 to $13 an acre for insecticide treatments to control rootworms, while a complete scouting package costs $6 to $7 an acre. The scouting service will look for rootworms and corn borers and will even provide weed scouting and a soil test."

But Larson's strategy doesn't end with three-quarter rates and scouting. He also studies the biological life cycle of problem insects and gauges when insect populations peak.

For example, to determine when the moths that produce corn borers will peak, he uses a blacklight trap and counts heat units.

The blacklight trap, placed in a grassy site, attracts the moths, which fall into a container and can be counted in the morning.

"We start looking for moth flights on May 1," Larson says. "And after we spot their first arrival, we start counting heat units."

With the heat-unit system, Larson determines the high temperature and the low temperature for every twenty-four hour period. Next, he adds the high and low temperatures, divides by two, and subtracts the result from fifty. He then consults charts that show the link between heat units and corn borer populations.

Larson also uses the biological insecticide, *Bacillus thuringiensis*, or *Bt*, on some acres to control corn borers. Biological insecticides are less toxic to both producers and the environment than traditional insecticides.

"You have to put *Bt* on earlier than conventional insecticides, and you have to be on top of scouting to use it," he points out. But the *Bt* has been successful enough that he plans to increase the number of acres on which he uses it.

Another new area under study by Larson is the use of beneficial insects to control pests.

"We try to select pesticides that do not kill beneficials," he says. "But research in this area is new. We still don't know what populations of beneficial insects are necessary to take care of pests. Not enough is known yet.

"These tools are all part of the puzzle," he adds. "Insecticides are part of the puzzle too, but they are only *one* part."

14 Consider using biological insecticides

Pros and cons

Biological insecticides are actual living organisms or the toxins produced by them. Examples include viruses, bacteria, fungi, and nematodes.

The chief benefit of using biological, or microbial, insecticides is their low toxicity to humans and nontarget insects. Some of these insecticides are so selective that they affect only one part of the life cycle of the insect, such as the caterpillar stage of moths and butterflies.

But there are drawbacks. Biological insecticides are sometimes more expensive than conventional pesticides because of the limited market and the high cost of developing, producing, and registering them.

Also, certain microbial pesticides can lose their effectiveness rapidly if exposed to heat and ultraviolet radiation, or when they dry out. For this reason, proper timing and application procedures are extremely important.

Some of these pesticides require special storage and mixing procedures, but this drawback usually inconveniences the manufacturer more than the farmer.

Biological insecticides for field crops

When looking for biological insecticides, keep a few points in mind:

- Most currently available biological insecticides are highly selective for the control of certain caterpillars.
- Biological insecticides probably will not control heavy pest populations, but they can control moderate populations of newly hatched worms.
- Biological insecticides must be ingested by the larvae, which will stop feeding within a few hours and die within two to five days.

What's available?

In many states, some of the biological insecticides available for use in field crops include Biobit, Dipel, Full-Bac, and Javelin. The common denominator among all of these products is that they contain the active ingredient *Bacillus thuringiensis var. kurstaki*, a bacterium.

The different biological insecticides may be formulated as dry or wettable granules, emulsifiable suspensions, or flowable concentrates. Crops on which some or all of these insecticides are registered include alfalfa, corn, small grains, sorghum, and soybeans. The insects listed on some or all of the labels are alfalfa caterpillars, armyworms, corn earworms, cutworms, European corn borers, fall armyworms, green cloverworms, and webworms.

As with chemical insecticides, it is extremely important to read the label of biological insecticides. The different products vary in terms of application rates, methods, timing, and placement.

Herbicides

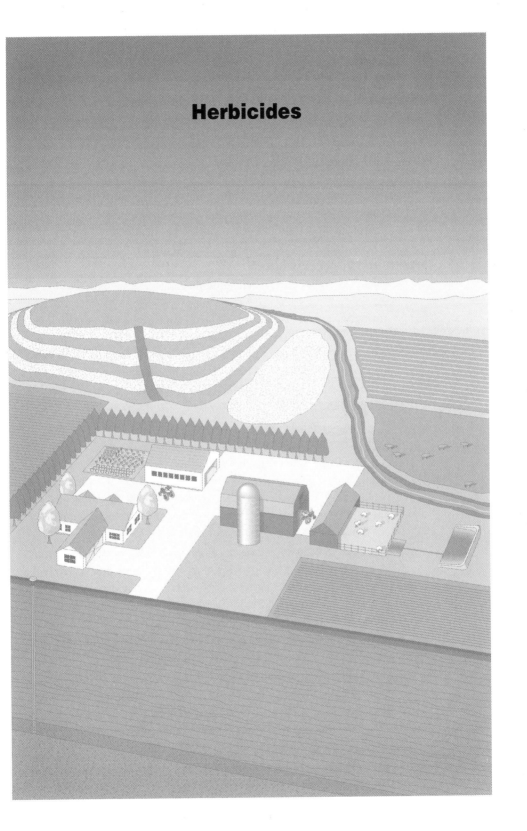

15 Know the economic thresholds for weeds

What is an economic threshold?

An economic threshold compares the cost of weed control with the money you would lose if you *didn't* provide weed control. It helps you determine whether there is a return on your weed-control investment. And it may help you avoid using unnecessary chemicals.

Determining the threshold

There are seven basic steps in determining an economic threshold for weeds.

If you must make separate herbicide treatments for grasses and broadleaf weeds, you should run through the seven steps twice—first for the broadleaf treatment and a second time for the grass treatment. However, if one herbicide treatment will handle both broadleaves and grasses, you only need to make one calculation. You can combine the figures for broadleaves and grasses.

Step 1. Determine the expected yield for the field. Use the previous field history and prevailing conditions to help you.

Step 2. Determine weed densities in the field for each type of broadleaf weed and each type of grass. To do this, scout the field 10 to 15 days after planting. For broadleaf weeds, count or estimate the number of weeds per 100 feet of row. For grasses, count or estimate the number of weeds or weed *clumps* per 100 feet of row.

Step 3. Once you know the average number of each type of weed in the field, refer to the two accompanying charts—one for broadleaf weeds and the other for grasses. These charts will tell you the percent of yield loss you can expect with different weed densities. If you are looking at the effect of more than one weed species, determine the effect of each weed species separately. Then add the different percentages of yield loss together.

Step 4. Multiply the percent of expected loss from the weeds by your expected yield. This will tell you what yield loss to expect *without* weed control.

Step 5. Determine the cost of yield loss without control by multiplying the expected yield loss by the expected cash grain price per bushel.

Step 6. Determine the cost of weed treatment, including wages, fuel, herbicide, additives, expected effectiveness of the treatment, and so forth.

Step 7. Subtract the cost of herbicide treatment from the cost of yield loss to determine whether weed treatment results in a net economic return or a net loss.

Important points

- If a weed is not listed on these charts, use data from a listed weed that has similar growth habits (size of plant, rate of growth, life cycle, time of emergence, and other characteristics).
- Weeds that begin growth four to five weeks after crop emergence typically do not result in crop losses. If the crop fails to develop a complete canopy because of adverse conditions, however, late-emerging weeds can cause losses.
- Weed seed production usually is not a concern if you typically use preplant or preemergence herbicides each year. However, weeds may cause more loss than indicated on these charts if you encounter perennial weeds and other problem weeds, or if the fields are only treated with postemergence herbicides.
- Scout weeds early (ten to fifteen days after planting) to improve the chances of control and timely application of herbicides. Scout periodically for four to six weeks.
- Conditions that slow crop growth and retard the canopy from closing quickly give weeds the edge. Under these conditions, weeds will have a greater impact on crop losses.
- Certain weeds may not cause economic damage but can still hinder harvesting. Consider this when deciding whether to control weeds.

Examples

Corn: You scout a field and find an average of 28 cocklebur and 50 pigweed per 100 feet of corn row. According to the chart, the cocklebur will cause a 6-percent yield loss, whereas the pigweed will cause a 4-percent loss. By adding the two yield losses together, you get a total loss of 10 percent.

> Expected yield: 150 bu/A
> Yield loss: 10%
> Expected loss: 150 bu/A x 10% = 15 bu/A
> Expected cost of loss: 15 bu/A x $2/bu = $30/A
> Average treatment cost: $10/A
> Net gain: $30 - $10 = $20/A
> Verdict: Treat the crop.

Soybeans: You scout a field and find an average of 8 giant ragweed, 25 velvetleaf, and 10 giant foxtail clumps per 100 feet of row. This translates into a potential yield loss of 8 percent, 4 percent, and 2 percent, respectively. Adding these values, you get an expected yield loss of 12 percent from the broadleaf weeds and 2 percent from the grasses. With available herbicides, broadleaves and grasses would have to be treated in *separate* applications, so you should make two separate calculations.

Broadleaf weeds

Expected yield: 40 bu/A

Yield loss: 12%

Expected loss: 40 bu/A x 12% = 4.8 bu/A

Expected cost of loss: 4.8 bu/A x $5/bu = $24/A

Average treatment cost: $12/A

Net gain: $24 - $12 = $12/A

Verdict: Treat the crop for broadleaf weeds.

Grasses

Expected yield: 40 bu/A

Yield loss: 2%

Expected loss: 40 bu/A x 2% = 0.8 bu/A

Expected cost of loss: 0.8 bu/A x $5 bu = $4/A

Average treatment cost: $10/A

Net loss: $4 - $10 = -$6/A

Verdict: Do not treat the crop for grass weeds.

Broadleaf weeds: Determining percent yield loss

Weed	Corn Percent yield loss						Soybeans Percent yield loss					
	1	2	4	6	8	10	1	2	4	6	8	10
	number of weeds per 100 feet of row											
Cocklebur	4	8	16	28	34	40	1	2	4	6	8	10
Giant ragweed	4	8	16	28	34	40	1	2	4	6	8	10
Pigweed	12	25	50	100	125	150	2	4	6	10	15	20
Lambsquarters	12	25	50	100	125	150	2	4	6	10	15	20
Velvetleaf	16	32	48	64	80	100	8	16	24	32	40	50
Morningglory	16	32	48	64	80	100	8	16	24	32	40	50
Jimsonweed	10	20	40	50	60	80	2	4	6	10	15	20
Smartweed	10	20	40	50	60	80	2	4	6	10	15	20

Grasses: Determining percent yield loss

Weed	Corn Percent yield loss						Soybeans Percent yield loss					
	1	2	4	6	8	10	1	2	4	6	8	10
	— number of weeds or weed clumps per 100 feet of row —											
Giant foxtail (5 to 8 stems per clump)	10	20	50	100	150	200	5	10	17	25	32	40
Shattercane (2 to 3 stems per clump)	6	12	25	50	75	100	2	5	8	11	14	17
Volunteer corn (up to 10 stems per clump)							1	2	3	4	5	6

NOTE: Grass seedlings may tiller soon after emergence. Therefore, it's often easier to count the number of grass *clumps* (rather than the number of single weeds) per 100 feet of row.

16 Fine-tune your weed-control program to reduce rates

Know the situation

Reducing herbicide rates requires that you know your soil, weed problem, herbicide, and equipment. Reducing rates may also require more time in planting and cultivation.

Listed below are a few strategies to consider.

Use herbicides that require lower rates

The most obvious way to reduce rates is to select some of the more recent products that can be used at extremely low rates. Instead of requiring rates that range from 1 to 2 pounds per acre, many new pesticides may be applied at rates as low as 1 ounce per acre or even 1/8 ounce per acre.

The major drawback to these herbicides is that most of them use the same mode of action. As a result, resistance may develop in some weed populations.

Consider adjuvants

Adjuvants improve the performance of postemergence herbicides, so using certain adjuvants could make it possible to reduce rates. It all depends on the adjuvant used, the weed species and size, and climatic conditions. Most adjuvants fall into one of four classes:

- *Surfactants* increase spray coverage and penetration.
- *Crop oil concentrates* increase the penetration of the spray through the cuticle (waxy layer) of the leaves. Because of this quality, crop oil concentrates work best to improve the control of "waxy" weeds, such as lambsquarters.
- *Liquid fertilizers* (28-0-0 and 10-34-0) increase the control of velvetleaf. When you're applying contact herbicides, liquid fertilizers are usually used in place of surfactants and crop oil concentrates. But when you're using systemic herbicides, it's usually better to add the liquid fertilizer to the surfactant or crop oil concentrate.
- *Methylated seed oils* are relatively new products. They are similar to crop oil concentrates but are more effective.

Know the impact of climate

In addition to being affected by spray adjuvants, postemergence herbicides perform differently under different environmental conditions. High temperatures and humidity may make it possible to lower rates. But weeds that develop under droughty conditions may need a higher rate. Also, heavy dew can cause the spray to run off when you add a surfactant.

Know the impact of crop rotation

A crop rotation makes it possible to include crops that require less herbicide—forage legumes, for instance. But even if you have no plans to include a forage legume such as alfalfa or clover in your rotation, crop rotation can make an important difference in herbicide selection. For instance, most of the newer herbicides that can be applied at very low rates are soybean herbicides. So a corn-soybean rotation offers a lot more potential for reducing herbicide use than continuous corn.

Spot-treat when possible

Irregular, localized infestations of weeds can be spot-treated with postemergence herbicides. "Bean buggies" and rope-wick applicators are ideal for maximizing control with spot treatments. New technology also makes it possible to spot-treat using electronic sensing devices that locate weeds and trigger the spray (see illustrations).

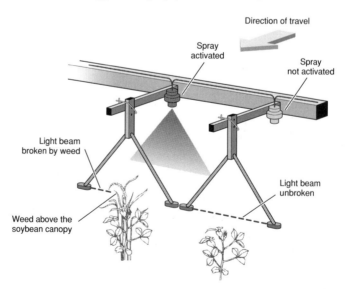

Direction of travel

Spray activated

Spray not activated

Light beam broken by weed

Light beam unbroken

Weed above the soybean canopy

New technology is making spot treatments more effective. For instance, this system uses an ultraviolet light beam to detect weeds sticking above the soybean crop canopy. When the weed breaks the light beam, the sprayer is automatically activated.

(Illustration adapted from materials provided by Progressive Farm Products, Inc.)

Consider split applications

Split applications may be more effective than single-pass applications, therefore allowing you to reduce rates.

Split applications make it easier to control both early-emerging weeds (lambsquarters, smartweed, and ragweed) and late-emerging weeds (cocklebur and morningglory). However, extra trips over the field cost time, fuel, and equipment wear.

Use herbicides in combination

When you use herbicides in combination, you often can cut back to 60 or 75 percent of the rate that is required when the herbicides are used alone.

Using herbicides in combination usually will not reduce your *total* load of herbicides. But it does make it possible to reduce the rate of a problem herbicide. If you want to reduce the rate of atrazine, for instance, use it in combination with another herbicide.

Herbicide combinations also reduce crop injury, carryover, or the potential for herbicide resistance.

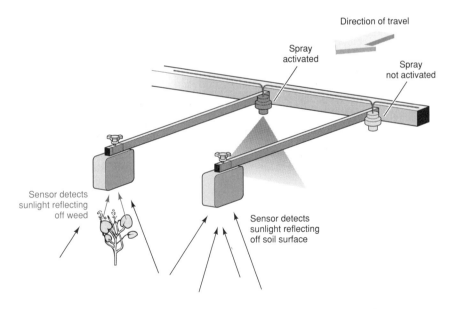

The light sensors in this system can distinguish green plant material from the soil surface by detecting different wavelengths of reflected light. When a sensor detects a plant, the sprayer for that row is activated and herbicide is applied directly on the weed as the sprayer passes overhead. A central control panel mounted in the applicator cab provides constant monitoring of sprayer activity. Because this equipment doesn't distinguish weeds from crops, its primary use is for preemergence weed control. However, researchers are studying ways to adapt the system for postemergence weed control in row crops.

(Illustration adapted from materials provided by Concord, Inc.)

17

Manage crops to compete aggressively with weeds

Standing up to weeds

When your plants thrive, weeds suffer. So anything you can do to help the crop compete aggressively with weeds will reduce your need for herbicides. Here are a few ideas.

Narrow-row soybeans

Planting crops such as soybeans in narrow rows makes them much more competitive with weeds than planting them in rows 30 or 40 inches wide. The narrow rows allow soybeans to shade their competitors earlier in the season, reducing weed growth.

However, if weeds do establish themselves in narrow-row soybeans and if control is necessary, you will not be able to cultivate mechanically. You will have to rely on herbicides. Therefore, going with narrow-row planting takes careful planning and consideration of the weed species present.

More oats

Planting oats at 3 bushels per acre, rather than at 1.5 bushels per acre, makes this crop much more competitive with weeds. But the higher planting rate is not useful if you are planting a legume companion. In this case, the higher planting rate would compete with the legume, slow the legume's growth, and perhaps reduce the legume stand.

Planting dates

Adjusting your planting dates can be an important way to reduce weed damage, but you need to consider the type of weeds you're up against.

In general, if you're dealing with early germinating weeds, such as lambsquarters or foxtail, give yourself enough time to control these weeds before planting. You may want to plant such fields last. Just keep in mind that delaying planting too long can lead to yield loss in corn and soybeans.

If you're dealing with late-emerging weeds, such as johnsongrass, pigweed, shattercane, or crabgrass, plant these fields first. An early planting will give your crop a head start on such weeds.

Other management pointers

- Keep in mind that the most important time for weed control in corn and soybeans is the first five or six weeks after planting.
- Plant early germinating hybrids that have good vigor.
- Fertilize to get the crop going.
- Use clean seed.

18

Don't increase herbicide rates with conservation tillage

Common assumptions

Time and time again, you've probably heard two of the most common assumptions about conservation tillage:

- Weed problems increase.
- Higher herbicide rates are needed to make up for the reduction in tillage.

The first assumption is sometimes justified. Although certain weed problems, such as velvetleaf, actually become less of a problem with reduced tillage, other weeds can proliferate—weeds such as fall panicum, marestail, hemp dogbane, and common milkweed.

But the second assumption—you have to increase herbicide rates—often does not hold true. University weed scientists say that even in no-till you should use no more than the labeled rate when applying any herbicide. In some cases, you may be able to *decrease* herbicide use in conservation tillage by taking advantage of certain cover crops or mulches. However, with no-till it may be necessary to use more combinations of herbicides, such as a contact herbicide plus preemergence herbicides.

It all revolves around timing. With preemergence herbicides, hit the weeds when they are small—no later than when the weeds start poking through. Also, use chemicals that have both soil residual activity and knockdown properties. Select some of the newer chemicals that can provide effective control at lower rates, and base your postemergence control on field scouting.

What about cultivation in conservation tillage?

With ridge till, of course, cultivation is necessary to create the ridges for the following season. Ridge till farmers in the Midwest have found that they can cut back on herbicide use significantly by banding herbicides over the row and cultivating between rows.

But what about with other conservation tillage systems—minimum tillage and no-till? Will relying on cultivation for weed control between rows be too risky?

Not necessarily. To find out how cultivation fits into your program, start with an area that can be covered in a few days. If the area were any larger, and if an emergency cultivation became necessary, weeds could get away from you.

Cultivation and residue

When cultivating in a residue-covered field, the key is to avoid clogging the machinery. Specially designed cultivators available today can handle residue. But if you have the common, sweep-type cultivator, you may have to make modifications. Conventional cultivators usually are equipped with five sweeps per row, so you may have to remove a couple of the sweeps to provide enough clearance for the residue to flow.

For more information on cultivator selection, as well as tips on banding and cultivation, see Chapter 19.

19 Band herbicides and cultivate

The cultivator strikes back

In the mid-1980s, many voices in the agricultural press began declaring that the cultivator was making a comeback. And from all indications, they were right.

Some farmers are looking to cultivation as a way to cut herbicide costs, improve profits, and reduce the risk of groundwater contamination. But much of its success depends on whether you broadcast herbicides or apply them in bands.

When herbicides are broadcast-applied, studies have generally shown that cultivation may increase yields on soils that form a tight surface crust by improving soil aeration and water infiltration. On some soils, however, cultivation does not improve yields when herbicides are broadcast and weeds are adequately controlled.

Cultivation looks more promising when you apply herbicides in a band over the rows and then use the cultivator to control weeds between the rows. Although the yield data are mixed, some studies suggest that the combination of banding and cultivation may give yields a small boost. Iowa State University research, for example, has shown that corn yields went up slightly when banding plus cultivation was compared with broadcast treatments.

In addition to the potential for increased yields, some researchers say that banding and cultivation can reduce expenses. They say that the reduction in herbicide costs more than makes up for the cost of additional cultivation.

As for erosion, cultivation again comes out looking good. University of Illinois studies indicate that cultivation can reduce soil erosion by increasing water infiltration and reducing surface runoff.

The risks

Cultivation is a time-consuming practice. If you cultivate at the wrong time or with poorly adjusted equipment, you can prune the crop's roots, bend and break the plants, or compact the soil.

If you depend solely on cultivation to control weeds, another potential problem is that rainy weather could delay cultivation during a critical time.

Selecting row cultivators

When choosing the right cultivator for the job, consider these options:

S-tine or Danish tine. This cultivator, usually equipped with five tines per row, is designed to operate at shallow depths and high speed in tilled soil with low residue cover.

C-shank (multiple shanks). The multiple c-shank cultivator has good soil penetration, is usually operated at a slow speed (2 to 4 miles per hour), and will clog when used in heavy residue. It is equipped with three to five shanks per row. Various sweep shapes and sizes are available and can also be equipped with weeding disks.

C-shank (single shank). The single-shank cultivator works with conservation tillage because a coulter to cut the residue is mounted in front of each shank. Each row assembly consists of a shank, with a sweep 16 to 24 inches wide and two weeding disk blades (or disk hillers).

The weeding disk blades may be positioned near the crop row and set to move soil toward or away from the row. Although the disk blades can be used to help build ridges, most ridging cultivators include ridging wings mounted on the c-shank, positioned in the middle of the row.

Rolling cultivator. The rolling cultivator uses two "spider" gangs on each row assembly. It will operate in high amounts of residue without clogging and can penetrate hard soils.

The rotary hoe

A rotary hoe consists of staggered, spiderlike wheels, spaced about 4 inches apart. The rotary hoe is a fast, economical way to control small weeds and break a surface crust to improve crop emergence.

The operating speed is usually 6 to 10 miles per hour, and the draft requirement is low. Rotary hoes, especially those with self-cleaning abilities, can be used in most conservation tillage systems.

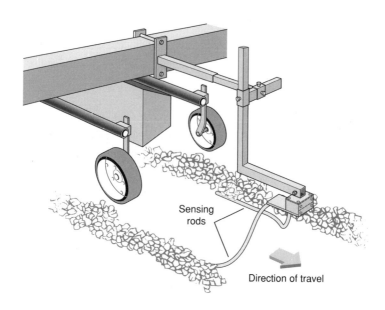

Sensing rods

Direction of travel

If cultivation equipment is poorly adjusted, you run the risk of pruning crop roots excessively or bending and breaking plants. A high-tech way to solve these problems is a system that automatically keeps the cultivator in line. With the system above, "sensing rods" run alongside plant stems, detecting the location of crop rows on both sides. This information is sent to an on-board computer that controls the tractor's steering wheel. If the sensing rods detect that the cultivator is getting out of line with the row, the computer automatically steers the tractor to correct the problem. Some versions of this row-sensing system move the cultivator from side to side, rather than steer the tractor.

(Illustration adapted from materials provided by Tri-R Innovations, Inc.)

Banding, cultivating, and watching the weather

John Burt says he has only one warning for farmers who are thinking of banding herbicides: "You have to be careful because you're at the mercy of the weather, and you're committed to cultivation."

Burt combines cultivation between the rows with banding herbicide over corn and soybean rows on more than half of his 1,500 acres near Pilot Mound, Iowa.

"Your cultivation has to be timed just right, because you only have a small window of time to get in there," says Burt, who usually makes one pass with his cultivator seven to ten days after spraying. "You could get caught in a wet spring after planting, but I've had no trouble so far."

Burt began banding preemergence herbicides in 1988, and after he saw the results he started banding postemergence a few years later. Not only has he maintained yields in the banded fields, but he also has cut his herbicide costs in half compared to broadcast. He uses a 12-inch band over corn and soybean rows that are spaced 30 inches apart.

"I look at each field, and I have some that are susceptible to weeds, and I have some where there isn't much weed pressure," he says. "In the ones that aren't so susceptible to pressure, I band and cultivate. I'm going more in that direction."

20 Control weeds with cover crops

What works best

Cover crops are often planted to reduce soil erosion during the winter and early spring. But if you manage cover crops properly, they may also help reduce weed populations. How much weed-control benefit you get from cover crops is a point of dispute.

The methods described below are all highly dependent on a variety of conditions, such as rainfall, temperature, and soil characteristics. Before beginning a cover-crop program, experiment with different management techniques and crop species to find out what works best on your farm.

In the Midwest, the cover crops with the best potential for controlling weeds are rye, wheat, and spring oats. Each of these crops has advantages and drawbacks.

Rye and wheat

Some studies have shown that after rye and wheat are killed, they release chemicals that may reduce weed growth. If you kill them a few weeks before planting corn or soybeans in the residue, rye and wheat could help you fight weeds.

Other researchers are not sure that the chemicals in rye or wheat effectively control weeds. What's more, some point out that the chemical released to fight weed growth can also hurt corn. But most agree that planting in the heavy residue left by these grasses will reduce weed germination and growth, as well as provide good mulch for your next crop.

One drawback is that rye and wheat take water from the soil. If it is a dry summer and you kill these crops too late, your cash crop could suffer from lack of moisture.

Oats

Oats planted in the fall can also reduce weed growth when crops are planted in its residue. But the protection is not as effective as with rye and wheat. The oats usually die over the winter and don't leave as much residue at planting time.

An oats cover crop can still help you, however, because the residue provides shade and mulch. Also, because the oats usually die over the winter, you don't have to worry that they will deprive your next crop of soil moisture.

Companion crops

Another type of cover crop is a companion crop, which grows alongside your cash crop and inhibits weeds that come up between the rows.

These crops are usually fast-growing, short plants that can quickly shade the spaces between rows while not seriously competing with your major crop.

Unfortunately, companion crops limit your ability to use many herbicides and eliminate the option of mechanical cultivation.

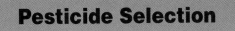

Pesticide Selection

21 Determine the organic-matter content of your soil

Organic matter and leaching

Organic-matter content is one of the most important but often overlooked soil properties. Organic matter is getting a little more respect these days, however, as its link with groundwater protection receives more attention.

Pesticides typically attach (adsorb) to organic matter, reducing the chances of leaching. Therefore, the lower the organic-matter content in a soil, the more likely a pesticide will leach and threaten groundwater.

But groundwater protection is not the only incentive to know your soil's organic-matter content. When the organic-matter level is low, there is also an increased risk of applying excessive amounts of pesticides and possibly damaging the crop. Therefore, some pesticide labels will list lower application rates for soils with a lower organic-matter content. Some pesticides are not supposed to be used at all when organic matter is below a certain level. For example, it is illegal to use certain herbicides when the organic-matter content is below 1 percent.

When you know your soil's organic-matter content, you know when you can lower rates, which means saving money.

Determining organic-matter content

One way to estimate organic-matter content is to determine the soil type and look up its properties in the county soil survey. To be most accurate, however, the next time you have your soil tested for fertility, check the organic-matter content as well.

When a lab tests for organic-matter content, it usually measures the level of *organic carbon* in the soil. Organic carbon is directly related to the level of organic matter in a soil.

If you decide to have your field tested for organic-carbon content, be aware that levels can vary within the same field. If one soil is clearly dominant in a field, test that one and gear your application rate to it. If several soils are dominant, test all of them. Then gear your application rate to the one with the lowest organic-matter content.

In addition to soil testing and soil surveys, another idea is to obtain color chips from your local Cooperative Extension Service office. Because organic matter is linked to soil color, you may be able to use these color chips to look at your soils and visually estimate the organic-matter content.

Other soil properties

Organic matter is one of the most important soil properties that affects pesticide leaching, but not the only one. Here are two more:

Texture. Texture refers to the relative proportion of sand, silt, and clay in the soil. Leaching is *more* likely in sandy, coarse, or light-textured soils. Pesticides are *less* likely to leach in fine- or heavy-textured soils, such as those with a high percentage of clay.

Permeability. Permeability refers to the ability of water to move through a soil. If a soil has low permeability, water from a heavy rain may pond on the surface. If a soil has high permeability, water flows through the soil more freely and may cause chemicals to leach.

For more details on how soil affects groundwater quality, see Chapter 22, which focuses on soil leaching potential.

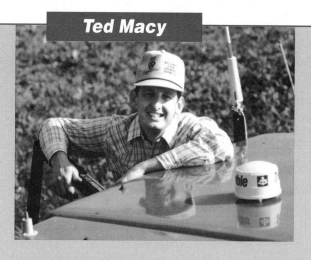

Ted Macy

Using high-tech to save $25,000 per year

By the turn of the century, the satellite system that helped American troops navigate the sands of Saudi Arabia during the Persian Gulf War could help farmers navigate their fields and apply the exact amount of fertilizer their crops require.

One of the people leading the charge in this direction is Ted Macy.

Macy says that 10 years ago he recognized the need to get away from uniform applications of fertilizers and pesticides on his 2,000-acre farm near Cambridge City, Indiana. Uniform applications across a field can't help but lead to over-application in some areas and underapplication in other areas. The result is less efficiency and more risk to groundwater.

To deal with the problem, Macy tried conventional controllers, which allowed him to vary rates manually. But the system lacked precision, so he became interested in computer-controlled systems that vary the rates automatically, according to needs in specific areas of a field.

By the fall of 1990, Macy was ready to try a "site-specific" farming system, which draws on the technology of both computers and satellites.

With this system, satellites send signals to a ground-based station, as well as to the tractor. In turn, the ground-based station transmits information to a radio control mounted on the tractor. All of this information makes it possible for a computer on board to tell the operator what area of land is being passed over.

Once the computer knows the field location, it can determine the fertilizer and pesticide needs for that spot—an area 1/1,000 of an acre in size. Then the system automatically adjusts the rate of application.

In 1990, Macy used site-specific farming to apply anhydrous ammonia in the spring and lime, phosphorus, and potassium in the fall. In 1991, he used it to vary rates of anhydrous ammonia, corn population, herbicides, starter fertilizer, and dry broadcasted fertilizer.

"In 1991, we estimated that we saved about $25,000 in input costs," he says.

This savings didn't include the cost to equip his two tractors with the system. But Macy says site-specific farming paid for itself in one year.

"For most farmers, they will be looking at a two-year payback or better," he adds. "Some companies estimate that you will be able to equip one tractor for $10,000 to $15,000."

With this kind of efficiency, Macy says the system should catch on rapidly when the first commercial units are available—possibly in 1993.

Macy had enough confidence in the system to retire from farming after the 1991 season and take a position with Applications Mapping in Frankfort, Illinois. Applications Mapping is one of the companies developing the technology for site-specific farming.

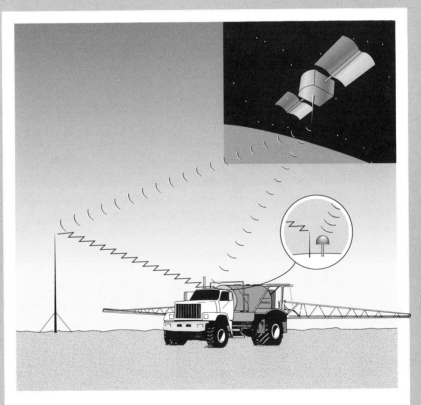

With some site-specific farming systems, satellites send signals to both a ground-based station and to the tractor. In turn, the ground-based station transmits a signal to the tractor. A computer on board the tractor pieces together all of the transmitted information to determine the exact location of the equipment. Then it makes automatic adjustments in the application rates of agrichemicals or even planting rates— adjustments tailored to that specific area of the farm.

22 Determine your soil's potential for leaching

The SCS connection

Earlier, we touched on several soil properties that affect the potential for pesticide leaching—organic matter, texture, and permeability. To get a handle on how these factors work together to affect pesticide movement, check with your Soil Conservation Service (SCS) office.

SCS has analyzed the characteristics of each soil type to determine the soil's potential for leaching. With this information, SCS places all soil types into one of four categories:

- *High* potential for leaching
- *Intermediate* potential for leaching
- *Low* potential for leaching
- *Very Low* potential for leaching

The categories for leaching potential may vary from state to state. Illinois and Iowa, for example, have only three categories for soil leaching potential. The "low" and "very low" categories have been combined into one category.

But what do these categories tell you? To answer this question, you need to take another step beyond finding out the soil's potential for leaching. You also need to find out the *pesticide's* potential for leaching (see Chapter 23). Then put both pieces of information together with the soil-pesticide interaction screening procedure (see Chapter 24).

The soil-pesticide interaction screening procedure looks at how the soil's leaching potential interacts with the pesticide's potential for leaching, and it provides you with a soil-pesticide interaction rating. This rating makes it possible to evaluate the overall potential of different pesticides to move to groundwater when they are placed on different soil types.

Which soil types do you focus on?

If one soil clearly dominates a field, select it as the representative soil type. If several soils dominate a field, determine the leaching potential for each one. Then gear your pesticide selection to the one that is most susceptible to leaching.

If the field has both fine-textured and coarse-textured soils, you may want to select two representative soils. Then determine soil-pesticide interaction ratings for both.

Determine your pesticide's potential for leaching

Pesticide pathways

When a pesticide is put down, it doesn't always stay put.

Pesticides can enter insects, plants, and other living organisms. They can volatilize, which means they change into a gas. They can be broken down by sunlight, microorganisms, or chemical reactions with water. They can chemically attach to soil and organic particles. And they can remain in a dissolved form, then leach with water through the soil, sometimes winding up in groundwater.

Many factors affect the risk of pesticide leaching. But here are some of the most important:

Pesticide degradation. This is the breakdown of a pesticide into compounds that are usually less toxic. The longer that a pesticide persists in the soil, the more chance there is of leaching. Persistence is usually measured in "half-lives." A half-life refers to the amount of time it takes for one-half of the pesticide to be degraded.

Soil adsorption. This is the attachment of a pesticide to soil particles, especially organic matter or clay particles. When pesticides attach more strongly to soil particles, they are less likely to leach.

Water solubility. This is the likelihood that a pesticide will dissolve in water. When a pesticide dissolves in water, there is more risk that it will be carried into surface water or leached into groundwater.

Volatility. This is the rate at which a pesticide will change into a gaseous form.

How do you determine the risk of leaching?

It's nice to know the processes that increase and decrease the risk of pesticide leaching. But what do they really tell you? How can you find out the leaching potential of your particular pesticide?

The following chart, developed by the Soil Conservation Service, takes many chemical characteristics into consideration and ranks pesticides according to their potential for leaching. The chart groups pesticides into four categories.

- *Large* potential for leaching
- *Medium* potential for leaching
- *Small* potential for leaching
- *Extra Small* potential for leaching

Keep in mind, however, that a *pesticide's* potential for leaching is just part of the picture. Another important factor that determines the rate of pesticide leaching is the soil type. Therefore, to get a more complete picture, you must also find out your *soil's* potential for leaching (see Chapter 22). Then put the two pieces of information together with the soil-pesticide interaction screening procedure (see Chapter 24).

Pesticide potential for leaching • Ratings as of March 1992

Herbicides

Trade name	Chemical name	Leaching potential
AAtrex	Atrazine	Large
Ally	Metsulfuron	Large
Assure II	Quizalofop	Medium
Balan	Benefin	Small
Banvel	Dicamba	Large
Basagran	Bentazon	Large
Bicep	Metolachlor + atrazine	Large
Bladex	Cyanazine	Medium
Blazer*	Acifluorfen	Medium
Bronco	Alachlor + glyphosate	Medium
Buctril	Bromoxynil	Small
Bullet	Alachlor + atrazine	Large
Butyrac 200*	2,4-DB	Medium
Canopy	Metribuzin + chlorimuron	Large
Classic	Chlorimuron	Large
Cobra*	Lactofen	Small
Command	Clomazone	Medium
Commence	Clomazone + trifluralin	Medium
Cycle	Metolachlor + cyanazine	Large
Dual	Metolachlor	Large
Eptam	EPTC	Small
Eradicane	EPTC + safener	Small
Extrazine	Cyanazine + atrazine	Large
Freedom	Alachlor + trifluralin	Medium
Fusilade 2000	Fluazifop	Small
Fusion	Fluazifop + fenoxaprop	Small
Galaxy	Bentazon + acifluorfen	Large
Gramoxone Extra*	Paraquat	Extra small
Laddok	Bentazon + atrazine	Large
Lariat	Alachlor + atrazine	Large
Lasso	Alachlor	Medium
Lexone*	Metribuzin	Large
Lorox	Linuron	Medium
Many names*	2,4-D ester	Medium
Many names*	2,4-D amine salts	Large
Marksman	Dicamba + atrazine	Large
Micro Tech	Alachlor	Medium
Option II	Fenoxaprop	Small
Passport*	Imazethapyr + trifluralin	Large
Pinnacle	Thifensulfuron	Medium
Poast Plus*	Sethoxydim	Small
Preview	Metribuzin + chlorimuron	Large

Herbicides		
Trade name	*Chemical name*	*Leaching potential*
Princep	Simazine	Large
Prowl	Pendimethalin	Small
Pursuit*	Imazethapyr	Large
Pursuit Plus*	Pendimethalin + imazethapyr	Large
Ramrod	Propachlor	Small
Reflex	Fomesafen	Large
Roundup*	Glyphosate	Extra small
Salute*	Metribuzin + trifluralin	Large
Scepter*	Imazaquin	Large
Sencor*	Metribuzin	Large
Sonalan	Ethalfluralin	Small
Squadron*	Imazaquin + pendimethalin	Large
Stinger*	Clopyralid	Large
Storm	Bentazon + Acifluorfen	Large
Sutan+	Butylate	Small
Sutazine	Butylate + atrazine	Large
Tornado	Fluazifop + fomesafen	Large
Treflan	Trifluralin	Small
Tri-Scept*	Imazaquin + trifluralin	Large
Turbo	Metribuzin + metolachlor	Large

*These ratings are estimates.
NOTE: A herbicide poses *less* risk to groundwater if it is foliar-applied, rather than soil-applied. Therefore, if any of these chemicals are foliar-applied, you can move it down one category. For instance, if the herbicide is foliar-applied and has a "medium" leaching rating, assume that its rating is really "small."

Insecticides		
Ambush	Permethrin	Extra small
Asana	Esfenvalerate	Small
Counter	Terbufos	Small
Cygon	Dimethoate	Medium
Dyfonate	Fonofos	Small
Furadan	Carbofuran	Large
Imidan	Phosmet	Small
Lannate	Methomyl	Large
Larvin	Thiodicarb	Small
Many names	Lindane	Medium
Lorsban	Chlorpyrifos	Small
Many names*	Diazinon	Small
Many names	Malathion	Small
Orthene	Acephate	Small
Penncap-M*	Methyl parathion	Small
Pounce	Permethrin	Extra small
Sevin	Carbaryl	Small
Thimet*	Phorate	Small

*These ratings are estimates.
NOTE: An insecticide poses *less* risk to groundwater if it is not soil-applied. Therefore, if any of these chemicals are not soil-applied, you can move it down one category. For instance, if the insecticide is foliar-applied and has a "medium" leaching rating, assume that its rating is really "small."

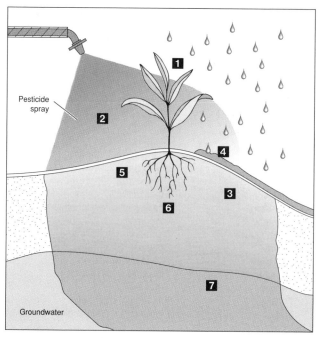

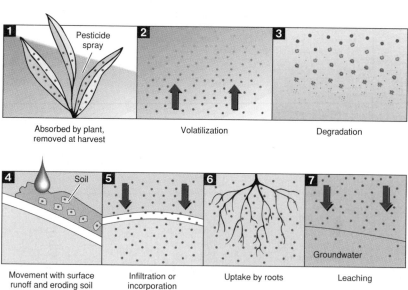

When a pesticide is applied, it can follow many paths. It can enter the plant, change into a gas (volatilize), break down into compounds that are usually less toxic (degrade), attach to soil particles and move with eroding soil, or dissolve in water and move with surface runoff. It can also move through the soil layer by either infiltration or through incorporation. Once in the soil, it can be taken up by roots, it can continue to break down, or it can leach, possibly getting into groundwater.

24 Determine the soil-pesticide interaction rating

Putting it all together

Once you know your *soil's* potential for leaching and your *pesticide's* potential for leaching, you are ready to put the two pieces of information together. You are ready to determine the soil-pesticide interaction rating.

By following the recommendations in Chapter 22, you should know whether your soil has a *high*, *intermediate*, *low*, or *very low* potential for leaching. You should also know whether your pesticide has a *large*, *medium*, *small*, or *extra small* potential for leaching. To see how these factors interact, refer to this chart:

Soil-pesticide interaction ratings for leaching

Soil leaching potential	Pesticide leaching potential			
	Large	Medium	Small	Extra small
High	High	High	Moderate	Low
Intermediate	High	Moderate	Low	Very low
Low	Moderate	Low	Low	Very low
Very Low	Low	Low	Very low	Very low

What the soil-pesticide interaction ratings mean:

High (potential 1). The pesticide has a high probability of leaching out of the rooting zone. To reduce the risk of groundwater contamination, consider using an alternative pesticide or another pest-management technique that does not involve a pesticide.

Moderate (potential 2). The pesticide will leach below the rooting zone more often than not. To reduce the risk of groundwater contamination, consider using lower application rates, other application techniques, or a different time of application. Also, consider using a different pesticide that has a lower potential for leaching. Additional on-site evaluation is necessary to determine how sensitive groundwater is to contamination.

Low (potential 3). The pesticide has a low probability of leaching out of the rooting zone. Minimize hazards by following the label.

Very low (potential 4). The pesticide has a very low probability of being lost through leaching.

NOTE: The categories for leaching potential may vary from state to state. Some states, such as Illinois and Iowa, do not include the "very low" category under soil leaching potential.

25 Consider other critical pesticide qualities

Three more factors

Whenever you consider the impact of a pesticide on groundwater, the leaching potential is the place to start, but it isn't the place to end your evaluation. Many other factors shape your decision about a pesticide's environmental impact. Three of the most important are the use rate, the toxicity to specific organisms, and the formulation.

Use rate

The application rate of a pesticide will greatly affect the likelihood that a pesticide will reach groundwater. Some of the newer pesticides on the market can be applied at very low rates, decreasing the risk.

Toxicity to specific organisms

When selecting pesticides, be aware of the plant and animal life in your area, and take necessary precautions.

An insecticide may have a low use rate and a low potential for leaching. But it is still the wrong choice if it is particularly toxic to honey bees in the area. In addition, a herbicide may have a low leaching potential, but it may not be appropriate if it presents a significant hazard to an endangered plant species.

Pesticide formulation

In most cases, different pesticide formulations do *not* pose different risks to groundwater—except in one case: microencapsulated formulations decrease leaching. However, microencapsulated formulations also increase the risk of surface runoff.

Pesticide Application

26 Select the proper nozzle tips

Expensive mistakes

Overapplying chemicals can be more expensive than you think. For instance, if a chemical costs $20 per acre, overapplying by 10 percent means you wasted $2 per acre. On a 500-acre farm, that adds up to a $1,000 error.

But overapplying farm chemicals not only costs you. Overapplying chemicals can also cost the environment. That's why it's so critical to select the correct nozzle tip.

To select the proper nozzle, you need to determine how many *gallons per minute* the nozzle must put out under your field conditions. Some manufacturers rate nozzles according to *gallons per acre*, but this rating is only useful if you operate under standard operating conditions.

Once you find out how many gallons per minute a nozzle must put out, find a nozzle that matches.

Selecting the right nozzle

Step 1. Select the spray application rate (in gallons per acre) that you want to use. Pesticide labels recommend a range of application rates for various types of equipment.

Step 2. Determine what the sprayer's ground speed will be in miles per hour, according to existing field conditions. Do not rely on ordinary speedometers as an accurate measure of speed because slippage and variation in tire sizes can result in speedometer errors of 30 percent or more. If you do not know the actual ground speed, you can easily measure it. (See the accompanying sidebar, "How to measure ground speed," on page 92.)

Step 3. Determine the "effective sprayed width" in inches for each nozzle. The effective sprayed width will be different for different spray methods:

- For broadcast spraying, the effective sprayed width equals the distance between nozzles.

- For band spraying, the effective sprayed width equals the band width.

- For row-crop applications, such as spraying from drop pipes, bander kits, or directed spraying, the effective sprayed width equals the row spacing (or band width) divided by the number of nozzles per row (or band).

Step 4. At this point, you should know the spray application rate in gallons per acre (step 1), the ground speed in miles per hour (step 2), and the effective sprayed width (step 3). With this information, a nozzle catalog can help you select a nozzle that gives the proper flow rate, measured in gallons per minute.

Step 5. If you don't have a catalog, you can figure out the required flow rate yourself. The flow rate in gallons per minute equals the application rate in gallons per acre (step 1) multiplied by the ground speed in miles per hour (step 2) multiplied by the effective sprayed width (step 3) divided by 5,940. Here is what that equation looks like:

$$GPM = \frac{GPA \times MPH \times W}{5,940}$$

GPM is the gallons per minute of output required from each nozzle.
GPA is the application rate in gallons per acre.
MPH is the ground speed in miles per hour.
W is the effective sprayed width in inches.

Using nozzles you already own

In some cases, you may not be looking for new nozzles. You may want to use nozzles that you already have on hand. If so, go back to step 2 and find out what ground speed will allow you to operate within the nozzles' recommended pressure ranges.

An even spray pattern means more effective pest control and less concentration of chemical in strips. To make sure your nozzles give out an even spray pattern, clean them regularly with a soft brush, rather than with abrasive objects such as a knife or wire.

HOW TO MEASURE GROUND SPEED

The easiest way to determine ground speed is to purchase speedometer kits that do not use drive wheels for speed measurements. These kits will give accurate measurements of ground speed. Radar and sonar are also accurate methods for measuring ground speed.

But even if you use speedometer kits, radar, or sonar, it's important to check these devices for accuracy. To do this, follow these steps:

Step 1. Lay out a test course in a field that has similar surface conditions as the field to be sprayed. Suggested distances for your test course are 100 feet for speeds up to 5 miles per hour, 200 feet for speeds from 5 to 10 miles per hour, and at least 300 feet for speeds greater than 10 miles per hour.

Step 2. At the engine throttle setting and gear that you plan to use while spraying with a loaded sprayer, determine how long (in seconds) it takes you to travel the distance on your test course. Do this again going the other direction. Then add the two travel times and divide by two. This will give you an average travel time.

Step 3. To determine your ground speed, you need two numbers to work with. To get the first number, multiply the distance of the test course (in feet) by 60. To get the second number, multiply the travel time (in seconds) by 88. Then divide the first number by the second one. Here is what the equation looks like:

$$\text{Ground speed (mph)} = \frac{D \times 60}{T \times 88}$$

D is the distance of test course in feet.
T is the average travel time in seconds.

Step 4. Once you decide on a particular ground speed, record the throttle setting and gear used.

EXAMPLE: You measure a 200-foot course. The first pass takes 22 seconds, and the return trip takes 24 seconds. You add the two travel times and divide by two. This gives you the average travel time—23 seconds. Knowing the average travel time and distance of the test course, you are ready to use the equation.

$$\text{Ground speed (mph)} = \frac{200 \times 60}{23 \times 88}$$

Calculations
200 x 60 = 12,000
23 x 88 = 2,024
12,000 ÷ 2,024 = 5.9

Ground speed   = 5.9 mph

27 Calibrate your sprayer

The next step

Once you have selected and installed the proper nozzle tips, you are ready to complete the calibration of your sprayer.

This is not a task that can easily be ignored. As the Alliance for a Clean Rural Environment reports, "Recent studies in several states have found that as many as one out of every three sprayers is miscalibrated by as much as 30 percent. Wrong pressure, wrong ground speed, and worn or damaged spray tips are common."

Check the calibration of your spray equipment every few days during the season or whenever you change the pesticides being applied. New nozzles do not lessen the need to calibrate because some nozzles "wear in," which means they will increase their flow rate most rapidly during the first few hours of use.

With the following procedure, you can check application rates quickly and easily.

Checking application rates

Step 1. Check whether the nozzles are delivering the required flow rate. (Determining the required flow rate is explained in Chapter 26, "Select the proper nozzle tips.")

The easiest, most efficient way to check nozzle flow rates is to purchase a nozzle flow-rate tester—an inexpensive item. A flow-rate tester is a vertical, plastic meter that you simply place under the nozzle and use to take a quick reading. It will tell you how many gallons per minute the nozzle is delivering.

It's okay if the flow rate varies from the required flow rate, as long as you know that and adjust for it. However, the flow rate for different nozzles should not vary *from each other* by more than 5 to 10 percent.

Step 2. Be sure you operate spray nozzles within the recommended pressure range. This is important because as spray pressures increase or decrease, flow rates change. (See the nozzle catalog to determine what spray pressure the manufacturer recommends.) Keep in mind that the range of recommended operating pressures refers to pressure *at the nozzle tip*. Because of pressure loss in the line and at check valves, the main pressure gauge at the controls may need to read much higher.

The easiest, most efficient way to check nozzle flow rates is to purchase a nozzle flow-rate tester. It will tell you how many gallons per minute the nozzle is delivering.

Step 3. Determine the amount of pesticide needed for each tankful or for the acreage to be sprayed. Add the pesticide to a partially filled tank of carrier (such as water or fertilizer). Then, with continuous agitation, add the carrier until it reaches the desired level.

Step 4. Operate the sprayer in the field at the application rate and ground speed that you selected, and at the pressure you determined in step 2. After spraying a known number of acres, check the liquid level in the tank to make sure your application rate is correct.

Step 5. Check the nozzle flow rate frequently. Adjust the pressure to compensate for small changes in nozzle output, which can result from nozzle wear. If the output is different from that of a new nozzle by 10 percent or more, replace the nozzle tips and recalibrate. Also, replace the nozzle tips when the spray pattern becomes uneven.

Calibrating and cutting rates in half

Precision pays.

Lowell Heap has found that if he examines his soil type, calibrates correctly, selects the right nozzle, and scouts weeds, he can cut herbicide application rates by as much as 30 to 50 percent—particularly on soil with high organic matter.

"But it takes confidence that you calibrated correctly and that you know your soil," says Heap, who farms 3,000 acres near Dewey, Illinois.

Heap calibrates his equipment every spring. If nothing goes wrong during the season, the only other time he needs to calibrate is whenever he changes products.

"If we are off more than a half of a percent, though, we re-calibrate," he notes.

To ensure an even, accurate application, Heap cleans the three main screens on his sprayer daily—the screen placed where water enters the system, the screen placed just ahead of the sparger tube, and the screen placed just ahead of the shut-off system. The screens in each nozzle only need to be cleaned once a year, unless a problem arises, he adds.

Heap cleans out the entire system by loading the sprayer with water and running it for almost an entire day. He does this two or three times before the farming season begins.

Keeping accurate measurements of every field is another important part of Heap's system, and he keeps this information in the tractor cab. That way, part-time help will know the exact size of each field. They will be able to mix the right amount of pesticide and end up with an empty tank when spraying is done.

If there is a little mix left in the tank, Heap dilutes it and sprays it on heavier soils, fencerows, and end rows. He says he never has any leftover mix that must be taken back for storage or disposal.

Whenever Heap changes systems or is using new equipment, he takes one other important precaution. He puts water in the tank and makes a test run, spraying 20 acres.

"That way, you will definitely know if you calibrated correctly," Heap says. "It makes me feel a lot better when I know I've got it right."

28 Consider direct injection

Technology with an impact

One study has indicated that a closed chemical mixing system can reduce your exposure to pesticides by as much as 99 percent. And one of the most popular closed systems today is the direct-injection system.

Direct-injection units can be equipped with multiple containers to hold different pesticides. The number of containers depends on the equipment. When you reach an area that needs an application of one type of pesticide, you inject that pesticide into the spray boom, where it is mixed with the carrier and applied to the field. When you reach an area that needs another pesticide, the flip of a switch transfers you to another container. The equipment injects that pesticide into the boom and applies it to the field.

Pesticides are only applied to the areas that need them, not to the entire field, so your total chemical use is reduced. This is good for the environment and good for your wallet.

With direct injection, the spray tank contains only water or some other carrier. Therefore, you don't have to worry that the residues of one pesticide will interact with the next chemical you put into the tank. Also, direct injection may eliminate the need to mix chemicals, so pesticide compatibility problems are eliminated.

When you are done spraying the field, simply remove the container, make sure it is properly marked, and store it until the next use. By using the same container for the same pesticide, you don't have to worry about leftover chemical, reducing chances of spilling and exposure. There is no leftover rinsate to deal with and no need to flush or clean the entire rig.

What's available?

Direct-injection equipment is available to both the farm-sized market and the commercial-applicator market. The type of mixing that occurs in the equipment depends on whether the pesticide is injected before or after the carrier pump. There are two basic systems:

- Pumps that inject the chemical into the spray boom or near the spray nozzle. They use an in-line mixer to properly mix the chemical.
- Pumps that inject the chemical on the suction side of the carrier spray pump. The pump is used to mix the chemicals.

The ability to control an injection system with computers makes direct injection an extremely popular way to apply pesticides. With computers, you can accurately control rates, making for more precise, site-specific applications. On-line printers are even available to produce a permanent record of what chemicals you used and where you applied them.

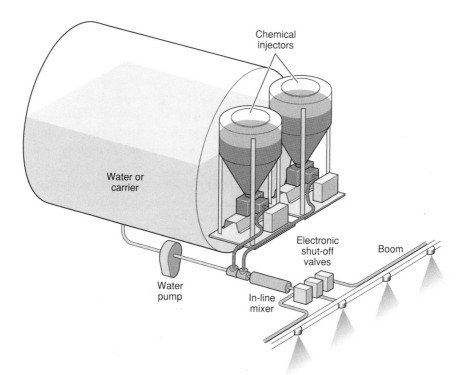

The direct-injection system allows you to mix the chemical with water or carrier in the spray boom, not in the tank. That way, you can apply different pesticides to different areas of the field—rather than applying a pesticide mix on the entire field. Direct-injection units come with multiple containers to hold different pesticides.

(Illustration used with permission of Raven Industries, Inc.)

29 Prevent backsiphoning

Simple solutions

Backsiphoning is the equivalent of pouring pesticide solution directly into your water supply. It is no minor problem. Fortunately, it is easy to prevent.

Backsiphoning can occur when you mistakenly leave the end of the fill hose *below* the level of the pesticide solution in the spray tank. If the water flow is inadvertently shut off, the pesticide solution could back up through the fill hose and get into the water supply.

To prevent backsiphoning, observe these precautions:

- Fill the spray tank with water first.

- Fill the tank from a hydrant that is at least 100 feet away from the wellhead. If the hydrant is closer, use a hose that is long enough to stretch at least 100 feet from the well.

- If you must add the pesticide first, make sure the water hose is secured above the tank and out of the pesticide solution. Maintain a 6-inch air gap between the hose and the tank opening. If necessary, mount a clamp on top of the tank to hold the hose.

- Always use anti-backflow devices, such as check valves, on pumping equipment. You can buy inexpensive anti-backflow devices from irrigation- or sprayer-equipment suppliers.

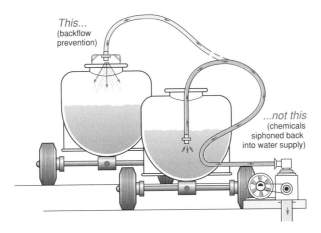

To prevent agrichemicals from backsiphoning into the water supply, always keep the end of the fill hose above the tank and out of the spray solution. Keep a 6-inch air gap between the hose and the tank opening.

(From *Protecting Our Groundwater: A Grower's Guide*. Used with permission.)

Pesticide Disposal and Storage

30 Rinse chemical containers thoroughly

Empty is not empty

Appearances are deceiving. Empty pesticide containers are not really empty. As much as 2 to 4 ounces of the chemical may remain inside an empty, unrinsed container. That's why an unrinsed container remains an unsafe container. An unrinsed container cannot legally be disposed of anywhere but in a hazardous waste landfill.

Although the technology is constantly changing and improving, there currently are three basic ways to make sure a pesticide container is properly rinsed—the triple-rinse procedure, the jet-spray system, and the jug-rinsing system.

With proper rinsing, your container can be disposed of in any landfill or other disposal site.

Triple rinsing

To triple-rinse a container:

1. Empty the container into the spray tank and let it drain for 30 seconds.
2. If the container is designed to hold less than 5 gallons of pesticide, fill it about one-fourth full with clean water. If the container is designed to hold 5 gallons of pesticide or more, fill it one-fifth full with clean water.
3. Shake or swirl the container vigorously to rinse all inside surfaces.
4. Empty rinsate into the spray tank and let it drain for 30 seconds.
5. Repeat the procedure two more times.
6. Puncture the bottom so the container cannot be reused.

Jet spray

Speed is the advantage of jet spraying, or "pressure rinsing," as it is also called. According to Southern Illinois University research, it takes about two minutes and forty seconds to triple-rinse a container. It takes about sixty-five seconds to rinse a container with jet sprays.

A special pressure rinse nozzle is required to jet-spray, but it can be easily attached to your pumping equipment.

To jet-spray:

1. Drain the container into the spray tank.
2. While the container is still on the tank, thrust the pressure rinse nozzle through the bottom of the container and rinse for sixty seconds. The

With the jet-spray system, an applicator thrusts a pressure-rinse nozzle through the bottom of a pesticide container. As the container is rinsed (usually for sixty seconds), the rinsate drains into the spray tank.

rinsate will drain directly into your spray tank.

3. Allow time to drain, then remove your clean container.

Jug rinsing

With jug rinsing, you do not puncture the container. Instead, you place the jug over a nozzle, which rinses it with a pressurized stream of fresh water. This system saves time when compared to jet spraying. Jug rinsing is also safer because it eliminates the jet-spray puncturing device, which has injured some farmers. However, you should still puncture the bottom so the container cannot be reused.

A few other points

- Rinse containers immediately after emptying them. Otherwise, chemical could cake on the inside, making the container harder to rinse.
- Do not dump pesticide container rinse water on the ground.
- Allow rinsate to drain into the applicator tank. If this is impossible, store it in a rinsate drum for later use in the spray tank.
- Take special care when rinsing suspension formulas. They tend to settle and harden in the container, so you may need to do extra rinsing.

31 Dispose of rinsed containers safely

Liquid formulation pesticides

When pesticide containers have been properly rinsed, they are considered nonhazardous material. In most cases, you can dispose of them in a sanitary landfill.

Most cases. Not all cases.

Some waste disposal operators will not accept pesticide containers. They do not want to take the risk that the containers were *not* rinsed. But there are a couple of things you can do to make the containers more acceptable:

• Be sure the containers appear as clean as possible.

• Puncture the containers on both ends.

Bags and boxes

Open bagged and boxed chemicals at both ends so the landfill operator can see that they are completely empty.

Dispose, recycle, reuse, return

Keep in mind that there are ways to avoid the disposal dilemma entirely. Here are four options:

Disposable packages. Some packages are designed to dissolve in the tank.

Recycling. Certain areas have recycling programs for pesticide containers. For example, an Iowa recycling program handles containers that have been pressure-rinsed by farmers. The plastic jugs are collected at county landfills, inspected, and shredded. The plastic chips are then used to create new pesticide containers.

Reusable containers. Reusable containers are usually only an option for applicators who use large volumes of pesticide. These "mini-bulk" containers typically hold 15 gallons and can be filled again and again. You need a separate container for each chemical.

Returnable containers. Some manufacturers allow you to return empty containers in the same way that glass bottles are returnable.

A few more points

- Always follow container directions for disposal.
- Before you throw away a container, make sure you cannot recycle or return it.
- If containers have not been properly rinsed, do not send them to sanitary landfills or other disposal sites. It is illegal.
- The threat to groundwater also makes it illegal to bury pesticide containers or other pesticide wastes in some states. Take the rinsed containers to a licensed sanitary landfill instead.
- In some areas, it is also illegal to burn pesticide containers or other pesticide wastes. Some pesticides produce toxic fumes when burned, which may be carried great distances in the smoke. For instance, pesticide containers and some pesticides can create dioxin—an extremely dangerous chemical—when burned. If you live in a state where burning is allowed and you decide to do it, stay out of the smoke and only burn on ground where the chemical was applied.
- Do not reuse pesticide containers for other purposes.

Dispose of excess chemicals safely

Solutions

Excess pesticide solution calls for solutions of a different kind. It calls for practical ideas on how to handle the following material:

Haulback tank mixes. This refers to unused pesticide mixtures left over from spraying operations. Pesticide mixtures may be left over for many reasons: miscalculations, misinformation, or interruptions in the spraying by weather or mechanical breakdown.

Rinse water. This is wastewater generated when you clean residues on the inside of spray tanks or nurse tanks. You need to rinse tanks at the end of each day and whenever you change pesticides, especially when spraying a crop that cannot tolerate the pesticide residues from the previous spraying.

Handling haulback tank mixes

Dealing with haulback tank mixes starts early on in the game. Only mix as much pesticide as you will need. This eliminates a lot of disposal and storage worries.

No matter how well you plan, though, you may still end up with excess chemical solution after spraying. If this is the case, apply the remaining solution to a field, *as long as it is in accordance with the label.*

Another option is to transfer a full or partial sprayer tank of material to a holding tank. Store the mixture for use at the first opportunity. Keep a thorough record of the pesticide concentration in the holding tank. That way, you can take into consideration the effect of this pesticide when making up a new tank solution.

Handling rinse water

Always flush out your spray tank at the end of the day or whenever you switch to another chemical. One way to do this is shown in the illustration on the following page. Attach a separate tank of clean water to your main spray tank so you can rinse out the tank when the spraying is done.

The rinsate from this procedure can be sprayed on the field as long as you don't exceed label rates.

If spraying on the field is not possible, store the rinsate in a holding tank. The best way to do this is to rinse your spray tank or pesticide containers on a rinse pad. Sumps would then direct the rinsate to the

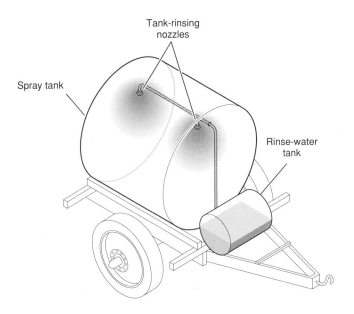

Tank-rinsing nozzles

Spray tank

Rinse-water tank

Attaching a separate tank of clean water to your main spray tank allows you to rinse the tank when spraying is done.

appropriate holding tank. You should have a rinsate holding tank for the corn herbicides and another for the soybean herbicides.

The next time you use the same type of chemical, you can use the appropriate stored rinsate as part of the carrier or mix water. The chemical concentration in the rinsate should be negligible as long as the recycled rinsate does not make up more than 5 to 10 percent of the next spray mix.

One last point

Consult the pesticide label for suggestions on how to clean the equipment. Some pesticides require cleaning solutions such as ammonia and water, or detergents and water, rather than water alone. However, beware of potential interactions between cleaning solutions. For example, mixing ammonia and bleach is dangerous because it produces toxic fumes. So follow directions carefully. Commercial cleaning agents are also available.

33 Store agrichemicals safely

Considerations

Whether you are looking for a new site to store agrichemicals or evaluating an existing site, consider several factors:

Residential, commercial, and livestock exposure. Locate the storage area as far away as possible and downhill from houses, children's play areas, feedlots, and barns.

Distance to surface water, sinkholes, and wells. Locate as far away as possible and downhill from these areas. Protect water sources from possible spills with a spill pad, buffer areas, and water-diversion structures.

Prevailing wind direction. Locate downwind from areas that would be most endangered by chemical exposure.

Fire hazards. Be aware of all electrical lines and connections in the area. Also, locate away from flammable structures and areas. If possible, make sure fire-fighting equipment can reach the building from all sides. A 12-foot-wide road is wide enough for emergency equipment.

Flooding. Do not locate in an area that is prone to flooding. Be sure the storage building site is at least 12 inches higher than the surrounding soil.

Local codes. When selecting a new site for your storage building, be sure to check with local zoning and building codes.

Decreasing the risk of accidents

To decrease the chances of an agrichemical storage accident, take these precautions:

- Be sure the walls and floor are made of materials that spilled chemicals cannot penetrate and that can be cleaned and decontaminated easily.
- Make sure the storage area has a secondary containment system to catch spilled chemicals for reuse or disposal. Also, putting a curb around the storage building will prevent spills or fire-fighting water from flowing out of the area.
- Purchase chemicals for a single season when possible.
- Store only clean, unopened packages, or packages that have been properly resealed to prevent spillage.
- Regularly inspect stored containers for damage, which could lead to leakage.

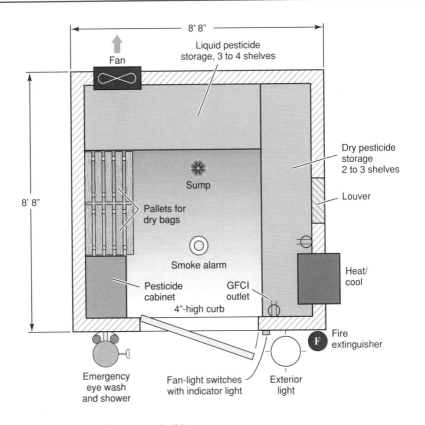

Plan for a small pesticide storage building
(Adapted with permission from *Designing Facilities for Pesticide and Fertilizer Containment*, MWPS-37, 1st ed. 1991, © Midwest Plan Service, Ames, IA 50011-3080.)

- Store herbicides, fungicides, and insecticides in separate locations of the storage area to prevent cross-contamination.
- Store dry, bagged pesticides on shelves or pallets off the floor to keep them dry. Also, store them above liquid pesticides to prevent contamination from liquid leaks. Store chemicals in glass containers on the bottom shelves.
- Do not store pesticides near food, feed, fertilizers, seed, veterinary supplies, and other products.
- Consider using steel shelves for storage because they are easier to clean in the event of a spill.
- Consider using shelves that have lips along the edges. This helps prevent chemicals from falling off the shelves.
- Lock, fence in, and post signs on the storage building to prevent accidental poisoning of children, livestock, and wildlife, and to deter vandalism.

This state-of-the-art storage shed includes many essential features: locked doors, warning sign, ventilation fan, heating unit, steel shelves, insulated walls to prevent freezing or excessive heat, and secondary containment system to collect spills. The storage shed also includes additional features, such as an eye wash, emergency shower, and explosion-proof lighting.

- Provide proper ventilation of the storage area to prevent the buildup of toxic or flammable gases and to keep the storage temperature between 40° and 90°F.

- If you don't have a secondary containment system to capture water, water sprinkler systems can cause more trouble than the fire they extinguish. That's because pesticide-contaminated water would have to be cleaned up. Dry-chemical fire extinguishers or similar systems may be recommended instead. Check with your local fire department.

- Develop a contingency plan with local authorities, such as the fire department.

- Have the proper cleanup and communications equipment easily available. Post emergency phone numbers where people can find them quickly.

- Keep a current inventory of all compounds. This information could be critical in an emergency, such as a fire.

34 Prevent and clean up chemical spills

Weighing the risk

Two pounds of pesticide, evenly distributed in an aquifer, could contaminate 10 million gallons of water. So there are strong incentives to prevent a spill.

Here are some tips on preventing agrichemical spills and cleaning up when one occurs.

Preventing spills

- Mix and load chemicals away from water supplies, including wells, ponds, and streams. Also, avoid sinkholes and abandoned wells that have not been sealed properly.

- Never leave a spray tank unattended while it is being filled. If the tank overflows, you may end up with contaminated puddles on the ground or chemicals in the nearest water source.

- Maintain application equipment to avoid leaky hose connections and worn spots, which could break and spill chemicals.

- Clean mixing, loading, and application equipment away from all water supplies. If possible, clean equipment over a concrete pad equipped with a sump to catch rinse water containing pesticides. The collected water can be used as a carrier in later pesticide applications.

- Use antisiphoning devices, such as check valves, to prevent the tank spray mixture from backsiphoning down the hose into a water source—a stream, pond, or well.

- Consider a closed-system mixer and loader. Closed systems meter and transfer pesticide products directly from the shipping container to the mixing or application tanks, reducing the risk of a spill. Closed systems often rinse the containers as well, and they provide greater accuracy in measuring the chemical dosage. However, mechanical failures such as hose breaks may occur more frequently with a closed system. Also, keep in mind that antisiphoning devices are still essential with a closed system.

- If you use an emulsifier or spreader-sticker, add it before the tank is full. These materials tend to create foaming, which could cause the chemical to overflow onto the ground.

Cleaning spills

- Under certain circumstances, you should report the spill to the proper authorities. The decision to notify authorities depends on the size of spill, what chemical was spilled, state regulations, and potential threats to human health or the environment. For instance, notify state and local authorities if the spill reaches a stream, pond, or other water source. To determine when you must notify authorities, check with your local emergency response agency.

- Always keep materials for containing a spill close at hand. Know ahead of time what to do to contain a spill of the particular chemical you're using.

- If you have spilled a liquid pesticide, cover the spill area completely with a material that will absorb the pesticide: activated charcoal, adsorptive clay, vermiculite, pet litter, sawdust, or specialized pesticide-absorbent materials. Use enough material to soak up the liquid. However, do not use sawdust or sweeping compounds if the pesticide is a strong oxidizer. This combination presents a possible fire hazard. The label or the Materials Safety Data Sheet for that product should indicate whether the pesticide is a strong oxidizer or highly flammable.

- Do not hose down the area. Water will simply spread the pesticide, creating a wider area of contamination.

- Sweep or shovel contaminated material into a leak-proof drum.

- In some cases, you should cover the area with a compound that neutralizes the pesticide. It all depends on the pesticide spilled, so contact the emergency response agency or the manufacturer to find out when to use a neutralizing compound.

- After removing contaminated material and possibly putting down a neutralizing compound, test the soil. If the soil is still contaminated, continue to remove contaminated material and put it into a leakproof drum. Then test the soil again.

- Dispose of the contaminated water or soil according to Environmental Protection Agency procedures.

Sources of information

Sources of information on handling spills include the following:
- The pesticide manufacturer
- The Materials Safety Data Sheet and the pesticide label
- Local authorities

35 Construct a rinse pad

Concrete reasons

The most obvious reason for installing a rinse pad is to prevent pesticides from moving off site. But that's not the only reason. Here are a few more:

- A rinse pad allows you to capture and recycle rinse water.

- Some insurance companies do not cover the cost of cleaning up a chemical spill, unless it is specifically mentioned in the policy. A rinse pad could prevent costly spills.

- A rinse pad reduces legal liability and the chances of being penalized if a chemical spill occurs. Penalties can be steep.

- Some dealers will not deliver bulk fertilizer or chemicals unless you have a rinse pad.

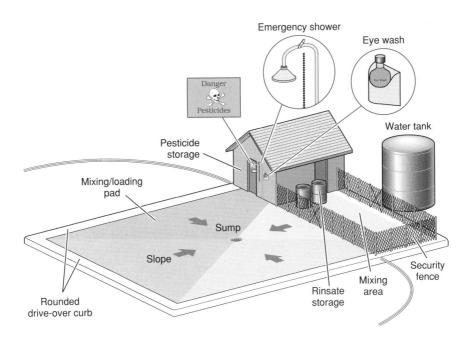

Rinse pad for small-scale, drive-across facility

(Adapted with permission from *Designing Facilities for Pesticide and Fertilizer Containment*, MWPS-37, 1st ed. 1991, © Midwest Plan Service, Ames, IA 50011-3080.)

Design ideas

There are many ways to design a rinse pad, but the best of them follow common guidelines:

- Locate the pad away from surface water and wells.

- Construct the pad from watertight concrete.

- Make sure the pad is large enough to hold your largest application vehicle.

- Design the pad so it slopes to the center and contains floor drains that lead to sumps. Sumps collect spills and rinse water, and they transfer the liquid to above-ground rinsate tanks.

- If possible, do not locate the pad in an area where mixing and loading has been done in the past. Constructing a pad in such an area might seal soil that is contaminated. If the pad must be located in an area where mixing and loading have been done, test the soil for contamination at several depths. If the test shows residual pesticide in the soil, remove the contaminated layer of soil before installing the concrete pad. This will help you avoid liability problems in the future.

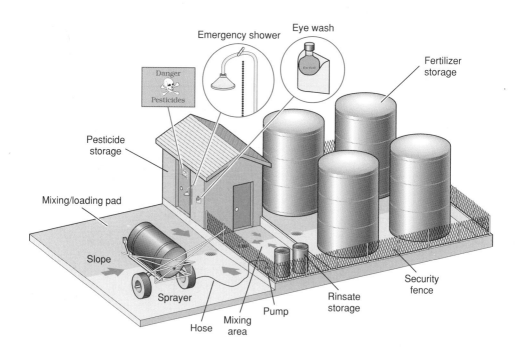

Rinse pad for a medium-sized facility

(Adapted with permission from *Designing Facilities for Pesticide and Fertilizer Containment*, MWPS-37, 1st ed. 1991, © Midwest Plan Service, Ames, IA 50011-3080.)

- Locate pumps and piping above ground and within the rinse-pad area.
- Make sure there is a level area for storage tanks at the back of the pad.
- Enclose the storage tanks with a low, concrete dike. Dikes should be big enough to contain an amount that is at least 10 percent greater than the volume held by the largest rinse-water tank. That way, the dike will be able to contain a serious leak.
- Store the various rinsates of incompatible chemicals in separate containers.
- Label rinsate storage tanks carefully so you don't mix incompatible chemicals.
- Be sure rinsate tanks are small enough to encourage the rapid reuse of rinsate material.
- Mount rinsate storage tanks 3 to 5 inches above the concrete floor. This allows you to spot leaks more easily.
- Keep undiluted fertilizers in a different containment area than undiluted pesticides. Each area should have a separate sump as well. You can divide fertilizers from pesticides with a concrete subdividing wall.
- For security and safety, enclose the undiluted chemicals with a fence and locked gate. If chemicals need to be protected from weather, keep them in a weatherproof shed.

Special note: These guidelines are aimed at small- and medium-sized farms. In certain states, some large farms are required to meet specific regulations. Check with your Cooperative Extension Service office, state Department of Agriculture, or Environmental Protection Agency to find out about state requirements.

Installing a rinse pad

When the local fire chief came out to the Melvin and Jeanne Stauss farm in 1989, the Stausses were in for a surprise.

"The fire chief told us that if we had a fire in the barn where our chemicals were stored, he wouldn't put a drop of water on the fire," Melvin Stauss says.

The fire chief explained that if a fire caused the chemical containers to melt down, any water they put on the blaze would carry chemicals into a pond, located 200 feet downslope from the barn.

The pond drains into a creek that runs through a nearby subdivision, then enters a stream and empties into Lake Michigan.

"It could be a total disaster," says Stauss.

The fire chief's news sent the Stausses into action. Today, the surrounding surface water and the groundwater below the Stauss farm is well protected with a 35-by-30-foot concrete rinse pad—big enough for their largest sprayer. On one corner of the pad is a 10-by-12-foot chemical storage shed.

Stauss and his son, Dan, farm 500 acres in Ozaukee County, Wisconsin. The operation includes soybeans, wheat, and pick-your-own strawberries, raspberries, and peas. They also grow sweet corn and peas for a canning company.

The Stausses' rinse pad and storage shed, designed with assistance from the University of Wisconsin Agricultural Engineering Department, includes these features:

The pad

- The rinse pad can handle a spill of up to 1,900 gallons.
- A 4-inch-high curb along the edge of the pad prevents runoff water from reaching the pad. The curb is rounded so vehicles can be driven onto the pad.
- Water drains to a shallow sump in the middle of the pad, where it is transferred to a rinsate storage tank.

The storage building

- The building has a 4-inch lip that can catch up to 250 gallons of spilled material. Any spilled material will drain into a sump in the corner.
- The building is ventilated mechanically whenever someone is in it and ventilated naturally whenever someone is not in it.
- An electric heater keeps the temperature inside the building at 50°F.
- A fire extinguisher, light, and emergency eye wash are located near the door on the outside of the building.

Other features

- Three rinsate storage tanks are kept on the pad next to the storage building. This is temporary storage for rinsate, which the Stausses use as make-up water when they are ready to spray the same chemical.
- The water used to fill sprayers is kept in a tank next to the chemical storage building. The tank is elevated so gravity moves the water to the sprayer. The water storage tank is filled by a water line from the barn, which is protected with a backflow prevention device. Also, the lowest part of the water tank is higher than the highest level of the sprayer tank. This prevents backsiphoning.

According to Stauss, the project costs were broken down this way:

Concrete work—materials and labor	$3,200
Building costs	2,100
Heating, ventilation, electrical equipment	1,300
Storage and pumping equipment, pesticide storage tanks, personal safety equipment, labor costs	2,600
TOTAL COST	**$9,200**

Since this was a demonstration project, Stauss says he only had to pay $1,000. Several Wisconsin agencies covered most of the costs, with additional assistance from Farm Journal Publishing.

"For some farmers, you may have to get the cost down more to interest them," Stauss says. "But you might be able to reduce costs if you went with a wood-frame building lined with steel. Our building is a prefabricated, all-steel structure. Also, the concrete might be cheaper in more rural areas than where we live." The Stauss farm is only 1 mile from the outskirts of Milwaukee.

Stauss says he has been surprised by the lack of problems to iron out. The only thing that hasn't worked is a sealant, which was put on the floor as an extra safeguard to keep chemicals from penetrating the concrete. The layer of sealant peeled off in a year. With that being the only problem, he says he is pleased with the pad and the storage shed. As he puts it, "It's a great insurance policy."

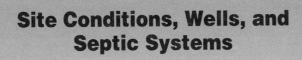

Site Conditions, Wells, and Septic Systems

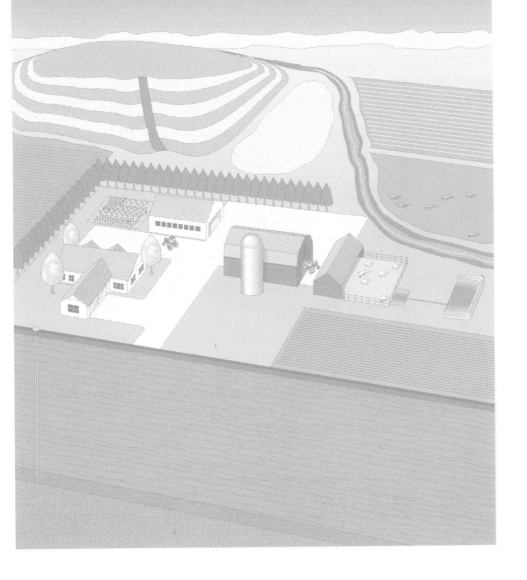

36 Know your site conditions

Groundwater mysteries

Most farmers have a good understanding of what's happening with their cropland—fertility, erosion, and pest control. But what goes on beneath the top few inches of soil is often a mystery. This is especially true when it comes to understanding groundwater.

Therefore, it's important to find out how characteristics of your land affect water movement and the risk of groundwater contamination. The major characteristics to consider are soil type, depth to aquifer, type of aquifer, other geologic conditions, precipitation, and temperature. Soil type was discussed in Chapter 22, but here is the rundown on the other site conditions:

Depth to aquifer

An "aquifer" is an underground zone saturated with water and capable of delivering water to a well at a usable rate. If the aquifer from which you draw water is within 50 feet of the surface, it is generally considered to be a shallow aquifer. These aquifers are more likely to become contaminated than deeper aquifers.

The best way to determine the aquifer's depth is to obtain a well log. If there is an existing well on the property, there should be a well log. If you do not have the log, check with the previous property owners or the company that dug the well. Otherwise, contact the state geological survey, state water survey, local well drillers, or your Cooperative Extension Service office.

Type of aquifer

There is a strong association between the detection of agrichemicals in rural wells and the type of aquifer from which water is drawn, reports a 1990 study by the Monsanto Company. The potential for contamination depends a lot on whether the aquifer is "confined" or "unconfined."

Confined aquifers. An aquifer is confined when it is bounded on the top by what is called an "aquitard"—geologic material through which water moves very slowly. This material, such as clays, shales, dense crystalline, and sedimentary bedrock, helps prevent contaminants from entering the aquifer.

Unconfined aquifers. An unconfined aquifer is bounded by permeable layers—geologic material through which water moves rapidly.

Generally, confined aquifers offer cleaner, safer water; but if chemicals should enter them, it takes a long time to decontaminate them. Confined aquifers may also be harder to find and can be expensive to tap.

Other geologic conditions

Regions with shallow limestone or dolomite deposits can be particularly susceptible to groundwater contamination because water may move rapidly through dissolved caverns or sinkholes.

Once water enters a sinkhole, it receives little filtration or chance for degradation of the chemical. Fractured rock systems also allow rapid movement of contaminant-bearing water.

Precipitation

In areas with heavy rainfall, a lot of water moves through the soil. Chemicals have less time to degrade because water will be moving through the ground more quickly, carrying some chemicals with it.

If the climate is dry and hot, there will be less water traveling from the surface down to the groundwater. However, heavy agricultural irrigation in these areas can greatly increase the amount of water moving through the soil.

Temperature

When it is warm, microorganisms in the soil actively break down pesticides and fertilizers. This can sometimes be beneficial because microorganisms transform pesticides into compounds that are generally less toxic. With nitrogen fertilizers, however, the breakdown process often poses *more* risk to groundwater. The microorganisms can transform the nitrogen fertilizers into nitrate, which can move more quickly into the groundwater.

The colder the temperature, the more these microorganisms slow down. In terms of breaking down nitrogen fertilizer into nitrate, research has shown that microorganism activity drops off sharply when the soil temperature decreases to about 50°F.

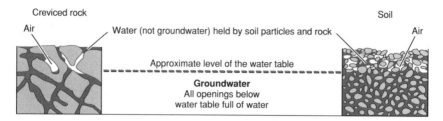

Creviced rock — Air — Water (not groundwater) held by soil particles and rock — Soil — Air

Approximate level of the water table

Groundwater
All openings below
water table full of water

When water fills all of the spaces between soil particles or rock, it is called groundwater. The upper level of the groundwater is called the water table.

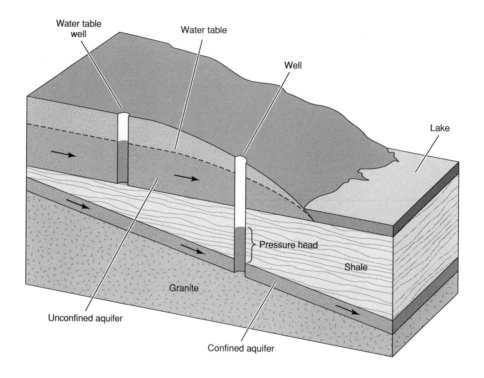

*An **unconfined aquifer** is bounded by geologic materials through which water easily moves. A **confined aquifer** is bounded on the top by geologic materials through which water moves very slowly.*

Because of the pressure inside a confined aquifer, the water level sometimes naturally rises in the well. This is called the "pressure head." With an unconfined aquifer, however, water in the well remains at the same level as the water table—unless it is being pumped upward. The water table is the upper level of the groundwater.

JOURNEY TO THE CENTER OF AN AQUIFER

Anyone familiar with Jules Verne's famous book, *Journey to the Center of the Earth*, may recall that his explorers found all sorts of oddities in the earth, including subterranean rivers.

When you journey to the center of an *aquifer,* however, don't expect to find a river flowing beneath the soil's surface. An underground river is a common, but inaccurate, image of what our groundwater looks like. In reality, groundwater refers to water found in the "saturated zone" of the soil. The saturated zone is where all of the spaces between rock and soil particles are filled with water.

An "aquifer" is a saturated zone that can deliver water at a usable rate. To put it in more visual terms, some have described aquifers as vast geological sponges.

Most aquifers recharge their water supply from surface water that trickles down through the soil. Unfortunately, as water moves between tiny soil particles in its slow journey downward, it can carry dissolved pesticides, fertilizers, and other chemicals with it. These chemicals usually attach to soil particles or are broken down by microorganisms in the soil. But they sometimes find their way into water supplies, especially if the water moves quickly through large cracks.

Beneath the soil surface, the movement of water is not simple and straightforward. Water doesn't just move straight downward. It often flows sideways, from higher to lower areas, and toward discharge points such as streams or rivers. It also tends to flow toward areas where groundwater is drawn up, such as wells.

The movement can be slow or fast. Water may only move a few inches per day, so contaminants may not show up in the water supply for days, months, or years after they get into the soil. In areas with limestone geology, water may move quickly through the ground. That is why it is important to study your site conditions carefully.

37. Evaluate your well location

A vital choice

Choosing a good site for your new well may be the most important decision you make in protecting your drinking water from contamination.

The decision may be difficult, however, because there are so many potential sources for groundwater contamination. But if you follow the general guidelines listed below, your chances of contamination will be greatly reduced.

Guidelines for choosing a well site

- Locate your wellhead on the highest ground available. This is no guarantee that water will be safe, though, because using a well creates an area of groundwater "drawdown." As the well pumps water from the aquifer, water beneath nearby fields moves to the well more quickly. Even contaminants in *downslope* areas may be drawn toward the well.

- Locate the well above the flood level of nearby surface water.

- Locate the well as far away as possible from potential sources of contamination, such as: barnyards; fields where chemicals have been applied; septic systems; storage areas for de-icers, road oils, animal waste, or other hazardous substances; agrichemical storage, mixing, and loading areas; fuel storage tanks; and landfills or land disposal areas.

- Check with county or state authorities to determine the proper setback distances, which are determined by the potential source of contamination.

- Check with local authorities or area residents who may know if there was ever a nearby dump site, underground storage tank, or other possible source of contamination.

- Ideally, place the well on the side of the contamination source *opposite* the flow of groundwater. In general, groundwater flows in the direction of a discharge point, such as a river, stream, or lake. This means you should try to position the well so the source of contamination is between it and the river, stream, or lake.

38 Make sure your well is constructed properly

Four points

Some problems with well construction are obvious: evidence of poor cementing or visible cracks in the casing, for instance.

But quite often, not-so-obvious problems are responsible for your water-quality woes. Therefore, whether you are designing a new well or evaluating the safety of an existing one, it's important to look at four main areas:

- Watertight casing
- Grout
- Watertight seals
- Graded slope

Watertight casing

The casing provides your well with a front line of defense against contaminants in surface water and shallow groundwater.

To keep surface water out of the well, the casing must extend at least 8 inches above the ground. If the area is prone to flooding, extend the casing 2 feet higher than the highest known flood level.

If a well needs to extend through a shallow aquifer to reach deeper groundwater, be sure the casing extends below the level of the shallow aquifer. Also, be sure the casing around your well is constructed of the proper materials. Steel pipe is used most often in small-diameter wells because it withstands stress during installation, pressure from surrounding earth, and corrosive soil and water. However, thermoplastic is becoming increasingly popular, and in some states it is now more popular than steel casing.

If the soil is particularly corrosive, stainless steel may be used. For large, bored wells, the casing is sometimes made of concrete or fiberglass.

Grout

There is usually a gap between the wall of the drilled or bored well hole and the outside of the casing. Grout must be placed in this gap or surface contaminants will move right down the side of the casing and into your groundwater.

Check with your state or county health department about proper materials to use. One common approach is to use a tight, cement-grout or bentonite-clay seal.

Watertight seals

All points where electrical wiring, pipes, or observation equipment enter the well should be properly sealed. Once again, if these points are left open, surface water or shallow groundwater can seep in.

Graded slope

A graded slope around the wellhead directs surface water away from the immediate area of the well, decreasing the chances of contamination.

Checking an existing well

When you inspect an existing well for proper construction, it helps if you have the well log—the record kept by the well driller. If neither you nor the well driller has the well log, check with your state geological or water survey. They may have a copy.

Next, take the well log to your department of public health, and they should be able to tell you if your well meets current construction standards.

Opening the well for repairs

Finally, remember that you must disinfect your well any time the system is opened for repair or a new one is installed. Typically the well contractor or pump installer is responsible for making sure this is done correctly.

WHAT TYPE OF WELL IS THE MOST VULNERABLE?

The news on large-diameter wells does not look good.

A statewide survey of Illinois wells, released in 1992, found that about 30 percent of the large-diameter dug or bored wells in the state had levels of nitrate-nitrogen exceeding the drinking water standard. In contrast, only 9 percent of the drilled wells exceeded the standard for nitrate-nitrogen.

The same held true for pesticide detections. Pesticides were detected in 23 percent of the large-diameter dug or bored wells and only 9.5 percent of the drilled wells.

In other words, well type *does* make a difference.

Here are the three major types of wells and an evaluation of how vulnerable they are to contamination:

Sand-point wells are probably the most vulnerable to contamination because they are shallow (typically less than 40 feet deep) and they are used in areas that have highly permeable sand and gravel aquifers. However, they are not as widespread in most areas of the Midwest as the other two types of wells.

Large-diameter dug or bored wells are also particularly vulnerable to contamination from sources near the well because of their design and generally shallow depth.

Deep-drilled wells are often not considered vulnerable to contamination from nonpoint sources of pollution. However, you should still evaluate the depth to the aquifer to get an idea of the risk. Also, a lot depends on the well's solid-steel casing, which keeps out shallow groundwater. If only a few feet of a deep well is cased, shallow groundwater may seep into the well. Shallow groundwater is more susceptible to contamination than deeper groundwater.

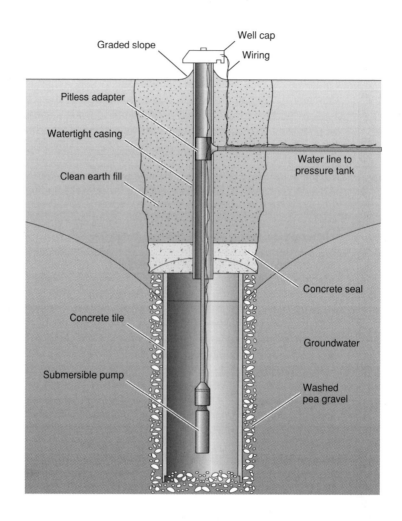

Large-diameter bored well

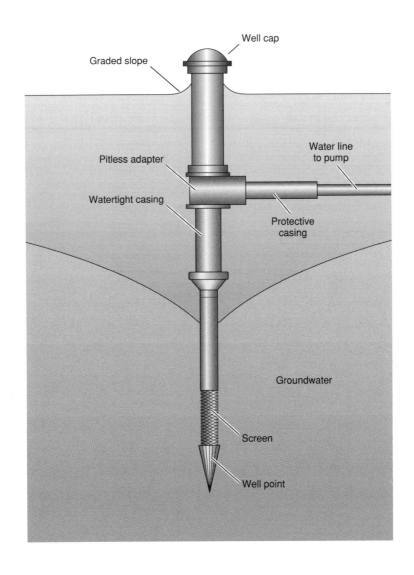

Sand-point well

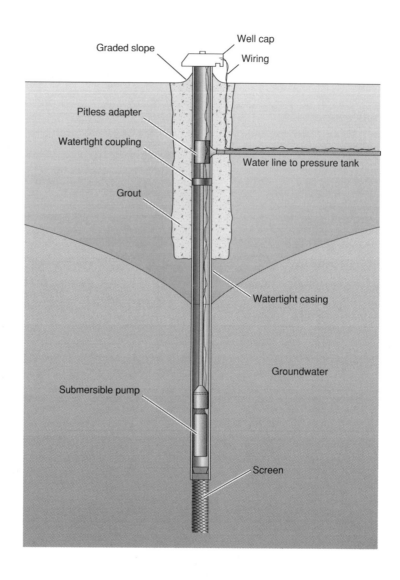

Graded slope

Well cap

Wiring

Pitless adapter

Watertight coupling

Water line to pressure tank

Grout

Watertight casing

Groundwater

Submersible pump

Screen

Deep-drilled well

39 Seal abandoned wells

The groundwater connection

Abandoned wells can come back to haunt you and your water supply.

Every year, many wells are abandoned when they are replaced with new wells or when homes are connected to community water systems. When an abandoned well is improperly sealed, or not sealed at all, it can be a hazard to safety and health.

Abandoned wells may provide a direct path from the land surface to groundwater. When they are not properly sealed, pesticides, fertilizers, and other contaminants have an easy path straight to your groundwater. You also run the risk of someone falling into an unsealed abandoned well.

In some states, sealing abandoned wells is required by law. Also, different states have different requirements on *how* abandoned wells must be sealed, so consult with your county public health department. Well drillers can perform the tasks required to properly seal an abandoned well. Other contractors may be able to do this work as well.

Locating abandoned wells

But what if there is an abandoned well on your land and you don't know it? Abandoned wells are not always in clear sight. To find out if there is one on your property, try contacting these sources:

- Former property owners or neighbors, who may remember well locations.
- Well drillers, who may be able to say where they drilled a well no longer in use.
- Old photos, which may show destroyed windmills, houses, barns, or other buildings where wells might be found.
- Fire insurance plan drawings, which might contain records of old wells.
- Government agencies or surveys, such as the state department of natural resources, water resource department, water management district, or geological survey.

40 Make sure your septic system operates correctly

The cost of malfunctions

A septic system is something you want to keep out of sight but not necessarily out of mind. If you don't maintain your septic system on a regular basis, the system could malfunction, possibly causing problems:

- Contamination of groundwater and surface water
- Spread of sewage-borne diseases such as cholera, typhoid fever, and, more commonly, gastroenteritis
- Costly damage to the home and septic system

The basic components

The most important factors in keeping a septic system operating properly are proper soil conditions, proper sizing of the system, and homeowner maintenance. Therefore, it's important to know the basic components of the system and how to keep them functioning properly.

Typical septic systems have two key elements—a septic tank and an absorption system. To get an idea of how these components work, see the illustration below.

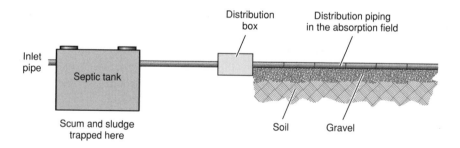

Septic tank. The septic tank is usually a concrete container that receives wastewater from your bathroom, kitchen, and laundry room. It allows heavy particles (sludge) to settle and light materials (scum) to float. In the tank, bacteria break down some waste products, allowing liquids to move into the absorption system.

The absorption system. The absorption system, or drainfield, consists of a distribution box, perforated distribution lines, and a soil area that has the capacity to accept wastewater. Wastewater from the septic tank moves through the drainfield, where harmful microorganisms, organic materials, and nutrients are removed.

Basic maintenance

To help your septic system operate correctly, follow these guidelines:

- Know the locations of all of the parts of your system, and don't run heavy vehicles over them.

- Avoid planting trees or shrubs near drain tiles. Their roots can clog drain lines.

- Divert surface runoff around the system, if possible.

- Be careful of what you dispose of in the toilet or in your drains. Household chemicals can destroy the bacteria that break down organic material in your septic tank; garbage disposals can add unnecessary solids and grease to your system; and non-biodegradable materials can clog the absorption field.

- Conserve water whenever possible. To avoid overloading your system on any particular day, try to distribute throughout the week your laundry and other chores that require heavy water use.

- Install a lint trap on the washing machine. Lint can clog the septic system.

- Monitor your septic tank annually, and have a reputable contractor pump it out every two to three years—or more frequently, if needed. Letting the tank overload with sludge reduces the time that wastewater remains in the tank. As a result, fewer solids settle in the tank, fewer solids decompose, and more solids reach the absorption field. Clogging the field with solids can result in premature failure of the absorption field and may require costly repairs or replacement.

Other systems

Systems that do not use a septic tank and absorption field are also suitable for waste treatment. Contact your local department of public health or Cooperative Extension Service office for information on installation and maintenance of other systems.

Water Testing and Treatment

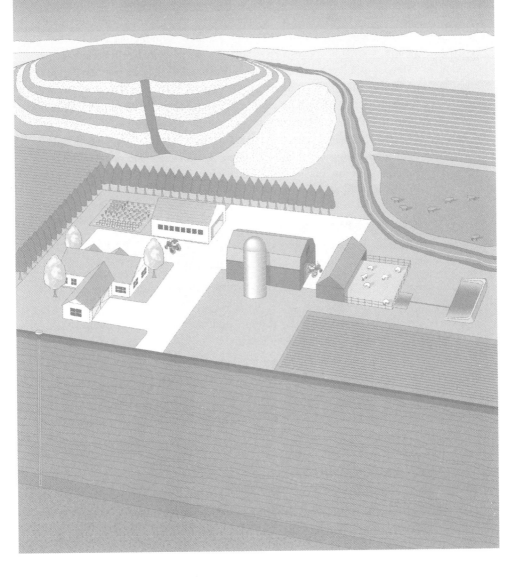

41 Test your water routinely

When should you test?

If you have a private water supply, you are your own regulatory agency. You are responsible for the quality of water that your family and guests drink.

However, contaminated water does not always look, taste, or smell different than safe drinking water. That's why you need to test your private water supply at least once a year—more often if problems arise.

People who get their water from a public or municipal supply have more protection because these supplies are governed by federal and state standards and are tested on a routine schedule based on the population size. But this does not mean people on public water supplies *never* have reason to test. It is possible that corrosive water or deteriorating pipes in your home may cause certain contaminants to get into your water supply.

The following guidelines describe conditions in which you should consider testing your water. The first section applies to people with a private *or* municipal supply. The second section generally applies only to someone with a private water supply.

Private or public supply

Reasons to test:

- Water has an objectionable taste or smell.
- Your household plumbing contains lead pipes, brass fittings, or lead-solder joints.
- The water leaves scaly residues and soap scum, or it decreases the action of soaps and detergents.
- The pipes or plumbing shows signs of corrosion.
- You are considering the purchase of water-treatment equipment, such as a water softener, iron-removal system, or water filters.
- You want to check the performance of water-treatment equipment that is in use.

Private supply only

Reasons to test:

- You have recurrent incidents of gastrointestinal illness.
- You are buying a home and wish to evaluate the safety and quality of the water supply.

- The water stains plumbing fixtures and laundry.
- The water appears cloudy, frothy, or colored.
- Water-supply equipment (pump, chlorinators, water heater) wears rapidly.
- You are pregnant, are anticipating a pregnancy, or have an infant less than 6 months old.
- You have a new well and want to evaluate it.
- Your well does not meet construction codes.
- Your well is in or close to a livestock confinement area. Check with your state to determine proper well setback distances for livestock confinement areas.
- You have mixed or loaded pesticides near the well.
- You have spilled pesticides or fuel near the well.
- You have had backsiphoning problems.
- Your well is located near an operational or abandoned gas station or fuel storage tank (buried or above-ground). Testing is particularly crucial if the tank has been known to leak.
- Your well is close to any of the following: retail chemical facility, gravel pit, coal mine or other mining operation, oil or gas drilling operation, dump, landfill, junkyard, factory, dry-cleaning operation, road-salt storage site, or heavily salted roadway.
- Your well is near a septic tank or septic system's absorption field. Check with your state to determine proper well setback distances for septic systems.
- You have a sand-point well, or a large-diameter dug or bored well. (These wells are more susceptible to contamination than other wells.)
- Your well is shallow (less than 50 feet deep) and one of these conditions exist: (a) the soil is sandy or (b) bedrock or sand and gravel is less than 10 feet from the surface.

If any of these conditions exist, consult with your local or state department of public health, state water survey, or a private testing lab to determine which tests should be performed on your water.

Who will do the testing?

The state environmental protection agency should be able to supply you with a list of certified water-testing labs in your area. Keep good records of water test results. That way, if you notice a change in water quality over time, you can better assess the situation. To obtain records of water tests by previous owners, Illinois farmers can check with the Illinois State Water Survey. The Survey has water-test results going back decades.

HOW TO READ WATER TEST RESULTS

Water test results express the concentration of most minerals in either "parts per million" (ppm) or "milligrams per liter" (mg/L). Don't let this confuse you. One part per million is equal to one milligram per liter.

Pesticides are rarely found in water at concentrations as high as parts per million or milligrams per liter. So they are usually reported in "parts per billion" (ppb) or "micrograms per liter" (ug/L). A microgram is equal to 1/1,000 of a milligram, and a part per billion is 1/1,000 of a part per million.

If it is difficult to understand what is meant by these extremely small amounts, here are some examples that may be easier to picture:

- One part per million is the equivalent of a teaspoon of soil dissolved in a pool of water 2 feet deep, 10 feet wide, and 12 feet long—about the area of a bedroom filled 2 feet high with water.

- One part per billion is the equivalent of a teaspoon of soil dissolved in water that could cover an acre of land to a depth of 5 feet.

Although these images emphasize how small the amounts being measured are, keep in mind that small amounts can sometimes have a significant impact on health.

For compounds other than minerals or pesticides, the results of a water analysis may be expressed in different forms of measurement. For instance, water hardness may be expressed in "grains per gallon," whereas the corrosion index simply estimates whether water is corrosive or not corrosive.

42 Test your water for coliform bacteria and nitrate

A tale of two contaminants

The two most common water contaminants are coliform bacteria and nitrate. Municipal water systems regularly test for these contaminants, but if you have a private well, testing for them is up to you. The good news is that most state and county departments of public health will test for bacteria and nitrate for free. Check to find out whether the service is available.

Routine testing for coliform bacteria and nitrate is a good idea, especially after a heavy spring or summer rainstorm. You should also disinfect the well and test the water any time you open the well—for example, whenever you repair or replace an old well or pipes, and after installing a new well or pump. Opening the well can introduce bacteria into the system.

If you are planning to have a baby, already expecting a baby, or have a baby less than 6 months old, test the water as soon as possible. Excessive nitrate levels in the water can be harmful, sometimes fatal, to infants less than 6 months old.

Bacterial contamination

Common sources of bacteria are livestock waste, septic systems, and surface water that gets into the well. Testing for coliform bacteria is important because it is an "indicator organism," which means that its presence may indicate the existence of other harmful bacteria in your water supply. Using an indicator organism is necessary because testing for all harmful bacteria would be difficult and expensive.

If your water test shows the presence of coliform bacteria, your water has some degree of contamination. However, the state cannot require someone with a private water supply to correct the condition. It can only recommend ways to correct or prevent the problem. The health department will recommend that you disinfect your water-supply system and then submit another sample for analysis.

The local department of public health, a licensed well driller, or a pump repairman can further explain the correct techniques for disinfecting a well.

Occasionally, public water supplies become contaminated with bacteria, and the supplier issues "boil orders." Boiling water is an effective way to kill pathogens (disease-causing organisms). Two minutes of vigorous boiling should effectively kill the pathogens.

Nitrate contamination

Common sources of nitrate in groundwater are fertilizers, septic systems, livestock waste, and naturally occurring nitrate in the soil. A water-testing lab will describe nitrate concentrations in one of two ways. The lab may describe the nitrate concentration as the amount of actual "nitrate" or as the amount of "nitrate-nitrogen." A nitrate concentration of about 44 parts per million (ppm) is the equivalent of a nitrate-nitrogen concentration of 10 ppm.

If unacceptable nitrate levels are found in your water, do not boil the water. *Boiling water does not eliminate nitrate.* In fact, it causes some of the water to evaporate, which *increases* the concentration of nitrate in the remaining water.

Use bottled water until you can treat the well water, eliminate the pollution source, or make repairs (if there is a problem with well construction).

Here are further guidelines on how you can use water that contains nitrate:

Nitrate guidelines		
Nitrate	Nitrate-nitrogen	Interpretation
0 to 44 ppm	0 to 10 ppm	Drinking water standard level. Safe for humans and livestock.
45 to 88 ppm	11 to 20 ppm	Generally safe for human adults and livestock. Water should *not* be consumed by infants under 6 months of age and pregnant women.
89 to 176 ppm	21 to 40 ppm	Generally acceptable for human adults and all livestock unless food or feed sources are very high in nitrate. Water should *not* be consumed by infants under 6 months of age and pregnant women.
177 to 440 ppm	41 to 100 ppm	Water should *not* be consumed by infants under 6 months old and pregnant women. Also risky for human adults and young livestock. Probably acceptable for mature livestock if feed is low in nitrate.
More than 440 ppm	More than 100 ppm	Water should not be consumed at all.

SOURCE: *Nitrates and Groundwater*, Kansas State University Cooperative Extension Service.

HOW TO COLLECT A WATER SAMPLE FOR BACTERIA/NITRATE ANALYSIS

If the local department of public health is testing your water, a representative is often willing or required to come out and collect the water sample. But if you are sending a water sample to a private lab, you may need to collect the sample yourself.

Fortunately, the job is simple and straightforward. When collecting a water sample to be tested for bacteria or nitrate, the Illinois Department of Public Health offers the following recommendations. (The procedure varies when collecting a sample for a pesticide test. It also may vary from lab to lab, so follow the lab's directions.)

- Collect and mail samples on Monday or Tuesday, so testing can be completed the same week.

- If possible, take samples a short time before the mail leaves the post office.

- Take the sample from a nonthreaded fixture, such as a bathtub spout.

- Do not take the sample from a fire or yard hydrant. Also, avoid swing faucets, faucets leaking at the handle, faucets that have attachments such as a hose or aerator, and faucets where food or beverages are dispensed or prepared.

- Wash hands before collecting the sample.

- Do not touch the inside of the lid or lay the cap down while collecting the sample.

- Let water flow for five minutes before sampling.

- Leave 3/4-inch to 1 inch of air space at the top of the bottle.

- Mark the date and time of collection. Then find out from the post office whether sending the sample special delivery will get it to the lab within forty-eight hours. If a sample is more than forty-eight hours old, it will not be analyzed. For best results, samples should arrive at the laboratory within thirty hours.

- If you live near the testing facility, consider hand-delivering the sample.

When testing for minerals in your water, collecting the sample is different in several ways:

- You may need to use more than one bottle.

- You may need to collect a sample at different points.

- When testing water for lead, you need to take a sample when water is standing in the plumbing and a sample when water has been flushed through the plumbing.

- A chemical preservative might be added to some bottles.

- Bottles are filled without leaving an air space.

Collect your water sample at an unthreaded faucet, such as a bathtub faucet. Also, do not set down the lid to the glass jar because it could pick up bacteria. For the same reason, you should never touch the inside of the lid or the sterilized jar with your fingers.

THE BLUE-BABY SYNDROME

The causes

Few cases of blue-baby syndrome have been reported recently in the United States, but the problem should not be taken lightly. Many doctors believe it is much more widespread than statistics indicate. They say blue-baby syndrome is often mistaken for other illnesses.

Methemoglobinemia (the technical name for blue-baby syndrome) usually happens when babies are fed formula made with well water containing high levels of nitrate. This syndrome is potentially fatal, so parents should have their wells tested for nitrate immediately if they have infants less than 6 months old or are planning to have a baby.

Before infants reach 4 to 6 months of age, bacteria in their stomachs can convert nitrate into nitrite. Nitrite enters the bloodstream and changes hemoglobin—an oxygen carrier—into methemoglobin, which *cannot* transport oxygen. As a result, the baby's body has a more difficult time transporting oxygen through its blood. In severe cases, the syndrome can cause death.

Doctors recommend that infant formula only be mixed with water containing less than 45 parts per million of nitrate, which is the same as 10 parts per million of nitrate-nitrogen. Some doctors also recommend that pregnant women avoid water high in nitrate because it may affect the unborn baby.

Symptoms

- Unusual blue skin color, similar to the color of blood vessels located close to the skin. The blue skin color may be especially noticeable around the eyes, mouth, and fingernails.
- Vomiting or diarrhea.
- Chocolate-colored blood.

Treatment

- If diagnosed early, simply using bottled water in the formula can stop the syndrome.
- If diagnosed in later stages, doctors may have to treat the baby.

Don't boil water

It's important to know that boiling water *does not* eliminate nitrate. Boiling water causes some of the water to evaporate, which *increases* the concentration of nitrate in the remaining water. To remove nitrate, use distillation or reverse osmosis. However, these systems can be expensive, so your best option may be to use bottled water.

Test your water for pesticides

Should you test for pesticides?

Do a little investigating. Find out whether any people in your area have discovered pesticides in their water. If someone in your area has confirmed well contamination, or if you are aware of a pesticide spill, have your well tested. You might also want to test if a commercial pesticide distributor is located nearby or if you have a shallow, large-diameter well, which is more easily contaminated than deep, small-diameter wells.

Find out what types and brands of chemicals are applied on the surrounding land or mixed at nearby commercial facilities. Testing for pesticides is more expensive than testing for nitrate and bacteria, so you want to have a good idea of what you're looking for. Then find a certified laboratory that will run those tests.

If your well is particularly vulnerable to contamination, you should not just test for pesticides once. You may need to test periodically throughout the year to get an accurate picture of the problem.

Finally, consider having your water tested for "degradation products" as well—assuming you can find a lab that is set up to make these tests. Not many labs are equipped to test for degradation products, which form when a pesticide breaks down. Degradation products usually are less toxic than the original pesticide, but sometimes they remain as toxic.

Testing for pesticides can be expensive, so consider it carefully and always ask for a cost estimate first.

Who can do the testing?

The local or regional offices of your department of public health will have information on where to have water tested for pesticides and may even be equipped to do the testing. Other testing facilities can be found in local engineering firms, water-treatment companies, and laboratories at local universities, especially in the departments of chemistry, agronomy, toxicology, or natural resources. A certified testing lab is strongly recommended.

It is usually best to have the water tested by a public or private laboratory that does not sell water-treatment devices. Also, beware of door-to-door water-treatment salespeople who perform on-the-spot water tests. These tests are not very accurate.

For more information on how to locate a public or private lab in your area, check the telephone yellow pages or contact your local Cooperative

Extension Service office, public health department, or Soil Conservation Service.

Once you have found a certified testing laboratory, find out what the charge is. Sometimes it is cheapest to have the lab "screen" one water sample for all of the chemicals you are looking for. Screening is an economical way to look for many chemicals, but it doesn't provide detailed information. Screening can detect contaminants but it cannot accurately determine their concentrations.

What if contamination is found?

If the test is positive for pesticides, you may want to immediately retest your well. Changes in rainfall, pesticide use, or water withdrawal can cause wide variations in the levels of pesticides found in your well.

A second test may give you a better overall idea of what is in your water. But always continue to test your water at least annually once any amount of pesticide is found in it.

If pesticides show up in your drinking water, it is important to contact a toxicologist with your department of public health. Another source of help is the National Pesticide Telecommunications Network, which has a toll-free number: (800)858-7378. The network system operates 24 hours a day, every day of the year. Generally, though, it's better to get help from authorities closer to home, rather than at a distance.

In addition, if you discover a problem, don't forget to contact other residents in your area who may be affected by the chemical contamination.

Health advisories

Once you know what chemical is in your water, and how much was detected, obtain a health advisory summary from the public health department or the U.S. EPA. Health advisory summaries will tell you the health effects of different chemicals in water. Unfortunately, though, many chemicals do not have advisories yet.

Health advisory levels are *not* legally enforceable standards. They serve as guidelines, and they contain a margin of safety.

The two-page health advisory summaries describe both the noncancer health risks and the cancer risk from pesticides and other chemicals. The summaries will either give you the "lifetime health advisory level" or the "cancer risk level," depending on what category the chemical has been placed in by the EPA.

The EPA categories are as follows:

A—Human carcinogen (cancer-causing agent)

B_1 and B_2—Probable carcinogen

C—Possible carcinogen

D—Insufficient data

E—Not a carcinogen

If the chemical is classified as "not a carcinogen" or a "possible carcinogen," the health advisory summary will give you the lifetime health advisory level. If the chemical is classified as a "human carcinogen" or "probable carcinogen," the advisory summary will give you the cancer risk level. Here is what those levels mean:

Lifetime health advisory level

When the level of a pesticide in drinking water is at or below the lifetime health advisory level, you can consume the water every day for an entire lifetime with a very low probability of increasing your health risks.

Cancer risk level

The EPA determines the cancer risk by using lifetime-exposure animal studies. Because the mechanisms that cause cancer are not well understood, the EPA uses a conservative method to determine the cancer risk level. Simply put, the cancer risk level is the amount of a substance you can consume every day and increase your lifetime risk of cancer by no more than one in a million—probably less than that.

What else do health advisory summaries provide?

Health advisory summaries also explain how a chemical is used, what specific health effects can occur, and what actions you should take if the chemical shows up in your water supply.

The likelihood of health effects showing up depends a lot on your health, how long you will be exposed to the water, how much the chemical is above or below the health advisory level, and whether any additional contaminants are present. Exposure to several hazardous chemicals can add to or sometimes multiply the effect of any single chemical.

How do you obtain health advisories from EPA?

You can obtain health advisory summaries from the EPA by contacting the Safe Drinking Water Hotline, Monday through Friday, 8 a.m. to 4:30 p.m., Central Time. The number is (800)426-4791. The hotline also provides details on drinking water quality and water-treatment methods.

In addition, concerned individuals should consult with their department of public health and their physician to interpret results and decide what to do.

MAXIMUM CONTAMINANT LEVELS

Although health advisories list advisory levels, they do not list maximum contaminant levels, also known as MCLs.

There is an important distinction between health advisory levels and maximum contaminant levels. In contrast to health advisory levels, MCLs *are* legally enforceable standards—at least for public water supplies. When a pesticide exceeds the maximum contaminant level in a public water supply, the public must be notified and steps must be taken to correct the problem. If a pesticide exceeds the maximum contaminant level in a private well, the homeowner is advised to correct the problem. But he or she is not legally required to do anything.

To obtain a list of maximum contaminant levels for different chemicals, you can contact the Safe Drinking Water Hotline at (800)426-4791.

Water standards as of May 1993

Pesticides

Common trade name	Use	Generic name	Lifetime health advisory (parts per million*)	Maximum contaminant level (milligrams per liter*)	Cancer risk
AAtrex	H	Atrazine	0.003**	0.003	Possible carcinogen
Roundup	H	Glyphosate	0.7	0.7	Insufficient data
Princep	H	Simazine	0.004	0.004	Possible carcinogen
Banvel	H	Dicamba	0.2	–	Insufficient data
Bladex	H	Cyanazine	0.001	–	Possible carcinogen
Counter	I	Terbufos	0.0009	–	Insufficient data
Cythion	I	Malathion	0.2	–	Insufficient data
Diazinon	I	Diazinon	0.0006	–	Not a carcinogen
Dual	H	Metolachlor	0.1	–	Possible carcinogen
Furadan	I	Carbofuran	0.04	0.04	Not a carcinogen
Lasso	H	Alachlor	–	0.002	Probable carcinogen
Lexone, Sencor	H	Metribuzin	0.2	–	Insufficient data
Marlate	I	Methoxychlor	0.04	0.04	Insufficient data
Milogard	H	Propazine	0.01	–	Possible carcinogen
Ramrod	H	Propachlor	0.09	–	Insufficient data
Sevin	I	Carbaryl	0.7	–	Insufficient data
Temik	I	Aldicarb	0.007	0.003	Insufficient data
Temik byproduct	–	Aldicarb sulfone	0.007	0.002	Insufficient data
Temik byproduct	–	Aldicarb sulfoxide	0.007	0.004	Insufficient data
Treflan	H	Trifluralin	0.005	–	Possible carcinogen
Several names	I	Chlordane	–	0.002	Probable carcinogen
Several names	H	2,4-D	0.07	0.07	Insufficient data

H = herbicide
I = insecticide
– No level has been established.
* Parts per million is the equivalent of milligrams per liter.
** Under review.

		Lifetime health advisory (parts per million*)	Maximum contaminant level (milligrams per liter*)	
Other contaminants				
Use	Generic name			Cancer risk
Component of gasoline	Benzene	–	0.005	Human carcinogen
Component of cleaning fluid	Carbon tetrachloride	–	0.005	Probable carcinogen
Antifreeze	Ethylene glycol	7	–	Insufficient data
Fertilizer	Nitrate-nitrogen	–	10	Under review
Fertilizer	Nitrite-nitrogen	–	1	Under review

LIFETIME HEALTH ADVISORY LEVELS (HALs) serve as guidelines, indicating when contamination levels could pose a health risk. They are *not* enforceable standards.

MAXIMUM CONTAMINANT LEVELS (MCLs) are enforceable drinking water standards for *public* water supplies. Although they are not enforceable standards for private wells, they still serve as important guidelines for those with a private source of water.

CANCER RISK indicates whether the chemical has been shown to cause cancer. A *human carcinogen* has been proven beyond a reasonable doubt to cause cancer in humans. A *probable human carcinogen* has been proven to cause cancer in laboratory animals, but there is insufficient evidence about its effects on humans. A *possible human carcinogen* has only limited evidence from animal studies indicating it is a carcinogen. It has *not* been proven to be cancer-causing in humans.

– No level has been established.
* Parts per million is the equivalent of milligrams per liter.

44

Know the signs of contaminants in drinking water

Tan water?

A mother in West Virginia looked at the tan water running out of her sink faucet and said, "Better than usual. Much better. Sometimes it comes out so thick it won't flow down the drain—just piles up in the sink."

As this example from an article in *National Geographic* indicates, some water problems are not hard to spot at all. But even when a problem is obvious, the cause of the contamination and the solution are not so clear.

The following list may help you identify what contaminants to test for. It concentrates only on those contaminants that leave sensory clues—taste, smell, and color. The list does not provide solutions, but it may help you select the proper water-treatment method (see Chapter 45). Also, be aware that if some of these chemicals are found at low levels in the drinking water, they may not leave noticeable signs. Even at low, unnoticeable levels, some of these chemicals can cause problems.

Contaminants that leave clues

If you notice...	Your water has too much...	Health effects
Grittiness, abrasiveness	Fine sand, grit	—
Cloudiness	Dirt, sand, clay, organic matter	—
Alkaline taste	Minerals	Effect depends on the mineral.
Black stains on fixtures and laundry	Manganese	Neurological effects at very high levels.
Blackening and pitting of metal sinks and fixtures	Hydrogen sulfide (gas)	Gastrointestinal problems
Blue-green stains on sink and porcelain fixtures	Copper, brass	People suffering from Wilson's Disease cannot excrete copper.
Brown-red water, stains, and discolored clothing	Iron	—
Chlorine smell	Chlorine/chloroform/chloramines	—

If you notice...	Your water has too much...	Health effects
Detergent smell (foamy water)	Foaming agents, dilute sewage	Risk of disease if bacteria present. Could harm infants.
Fishy, sweet perfume odor	Volatile organic compounds or semivolatile compounds	Risk of cancer. Could affect kidney, liver, or central nervous system.
Milky water	Any type of particles, air, methane	—
Metallic taste	Iron, manganese, copper, lead, or other metals	Nervous system disorders from lead, mercury, arsenic. Possible cancer risk from nickel, arsenic, chromium.
Musty, earthy smell	Organic matter (leaves, algae)	—
Oil or gas smell	Gasoline or semivolatile compounds	Risk of cancer. Could affect kidney, liver, or central nervous system.
Rotten egg smell	Hydrogen sulfide (gas)	Gastrointestinal problems
Salty, brackish taste and pitting of fixtures	Sodium, chloride, sulfate, inorganic salts	Sodium can cause problems for people with hypertension. Sulfate can cause gastrointestinal problems.
Sharp chemical taste or odor, or "oily" consistency	Pesticides or semivolatile compounds	Risk of cancer. Could affect any bodily organ system.
Soap curd, scum, white deposits in pipes, kettle, water heater	Hard water (water with dissolved minerals, such as calcium or magnesium)	Suspected link with cardiovascular diseases.
Staining and pitting of teeth	Fluoride	Bone brittleness, tooth enamel damage
Yellow water	Tannins from organic soil and vegetation	—

SOURCE: Adapted with permission from Water "Sense" Wheel™, © 1991, EHMI. All rights reserved. Environmental Hazards Management Institute, P.O. Box 932, Durham, NH 03824, (603)868-1496.

45

Select effective water-treatment methods

Treatment time

If you identify the contaminants in your water supply and determine that contamination levels exceed standards or guidelines, it is time to do something. You may be able to solve the problem by taking a look at the well's construction and determining whether repairs or replacement are in order. If correcting well deficiencies isn't the answer, consider a water-treatment method.

Make sure you know exactly what contaminants you want to get rid of, as well as your financial limits. Consult with water-treatment specialists and local officials. Also, do *not* have your water tested by someone in the business of selling treatment devices. And keep these points in mind:

- No single water-treatment system corrects all water-quality problems.
- All systems have limitations and life expectancies.
- All systems require routine maintenance, monitoring, or both.

The following guide is intended only to give you a general idea of the available technology. This guide tells you what contaminants each system can remove. But keep in mind that each system does not work with equal efficiency on all of the contaminants listed.

Major treatment methods

Distillation

Removes: Radium, odor, off-tastes, heavy metals, nitrate, and salt. Units with volatile gas vents can remove some volatile organic chemicals as well.

How it works: Impurities are removed when water is evaporated. Then steam is cooled and transformed into distilled water.

Limitations: The distillation process is slow and consumes a lot of energy, making it expensive. It also consumes large amounts of water if the coolant used in the distillation process is water. Distilled water can corrode materials such as iron and copper.

Air stripping

Removes: Gases such as radon, hydrogen sulfide, and methane. In addition, air stripping removes many volatile organic chemicals and helps treat some odor and taste problems.

How it works: Water flows down a tube while air is pumped up. Contaminants are transferred from the water to the air and then vented outside.

Limitations: Energy costs can increase because you repump the water after treatment and you must power the fan that blows air through the water. Also, units may be noisy and bacterial growth may occur in the water-holding tank. Air stripping is generally not used for private water systems.

Activated carbon filters

Removes: Many volatile organic chemicals, some pesticides, radon gas, and mercury. Also treats odor, color, and taste problems (such as residual chlorine).

How it works: Water is filtered through carbon granules.

Limitations: If the filter is not replaced regularly, it will lose its ability to filter contaminants. As a result, the contaminants may reenter the water in amounts that are even more concentrated than before. Infrequently maintained filters are also breeding grounds for bacteria.

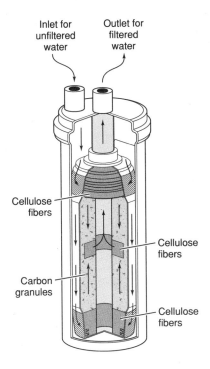

With an activated carbon filter, water enters the top of the cartridge. As water passes through carbon granules, certain contaminants attach to the surface of the material and are removed from the water. Water then moves up through cellulose filters to the outlet.

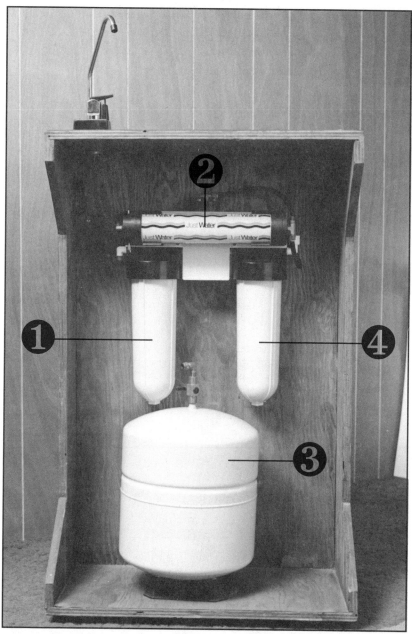

With reverse osmosis, water passes through a sediment filter ❶, which removes coarse particles that could clog the unit. Water is then forced through the reverse-osmosis membrane ❷, leaving contaminants behind. Contaminated water drains away and treated water moves to the holding tank ❸. When water is withdrawn, it moves from the holding tank, through an activated carbon filter ❹, to the faucet.

Some systems do not include an activated carbon filter, and some systems have an activated carbon filter placed **before** the reverse-osmosis membrane.

Reverse osmosis

Removes: Inorganic minerals such as radium, sulfate, calcium, magnesium, potassium, nitrate, fluoride, boron, and phosphorus. It also helps remove salts, certain detergents, volatile organic contaminants, pesticides, and taste- and odor-producing chemicals.

How it works: A membrane filters out dissolved impurities.

Limitations: Under-the-sink installations are costly and take up a lot of space. Costly filter replacement. Slow and wasteful of water. For every gallon of drinkable water, 4 to 6 gallons go down the drain. Some bacteria may be small enough to pass through the reverse osmosis membrane and colonize the holding tank.

Cation or anion exchange *(water softener)*

Removes: Barium, radium, and taste-, color-, and odor-producing chemicals. Water softeners will remove dissolved iron and manganese when they are present in low concentrations. Also, anion exchange units will remove nitrate, but cation exchange units will *not*.

How it works: As hard water passes through resin beads, magnesium and calcium ions attach to the beads and are removed from water. This softens water.

Limitations: People with hypertension or high blood pressure should consult their doctor about possible health risks associated with drinking softened water. Sodium is normally added to water during the softening process and can cause health problems for these people. Remember, cation and anion exchange softeners are different types of water softeners and remove different minerals.

Mechanical filtration

Removes: Dirt, sediment, loose scale, and insoluble iron and manganese (flakes that have not dissolved).

How it works: Sand, filter paper, compressed glass wool, or other straining material clears the water of dirt, sediment, and other particles.

Limitations: Mechanical filtration does not do much to remove harmful, dissolved chemicals.

Chlorination

Removes: Bacteria, other microbiological contaminants, and some taste-, odor-, and color-producing chemicals. Chlorinators also remove hydrogen sulfide and dissolved iron and manganese when followed by mechanical filtration or an activated carbon filter.

How it works: A pump feeds chlorine into the water. The pump can dispense chlorine in direct proportion to the rate of water flow. Chlorine has a residual effect, which means it works for a while after being added to the water.

Limitations: If the system is not operated properly, it is expensive and possibly toxic. Chlorination by-products may be harmful.

Ultraviolet radiation

Removes: Bacteria and other microbiological contaminants.

How it works: As water passes by a special light bulb, ultraviolet radiation kills contaminants.

Limitations: May not work effectively in cloudy water or when the water flow is too fast. Unless the unit is equipped with a special meter, it is hard to know whether the system is doing the job. UV units do not have a residual effect, as chlorination does.

Ozonation

Removes: Bacteria, other microbiological contaminants, and some taste-, odor-, and color-producing chemicals. Ozonation also removes hydrogen sulfide and dissolved iron and manganese when followed by mechanical filtration or an activated carbon filter.

How it works: Water is exposed to ozone gas, which destroys microorganisms.

Limitations: Equipment to generate ozone is expensive. Ozonation does not have a residual effect, as chlorination does.

Oxidizing filters *(greensand filters or zeolite filters)*

Removes: Iron, manganese, and hydrogen sulfide.

How it works: Contaminants are removed through filtering and chemical reactions.

Limitations: The system needs to be regenerated with potassium permanganate, which is a hazard to eyes and skin.

Treatment Methods

Contaminants	Activated carbon filters	Air stripping	Chlorination	Distillation	Cation or anion exchange/water softener	Mechanical filtration	Reverse osmosis	Ultraviolet radiation	Ozonation	Oxidizing filters
Chlorine	X									
Coliform bacteria, other microorganisms			X					X	X	
Color	X		X		X				X	
Hydrogen sulfide		X	X [1]						X [1]	X
Inorganics, minerals, and heavy metals (lead, mercury, arsenic, cadmium, barium)	X [2]			X	X [3]		X			
Iron/manganese – dissolved			X [1]		X [4]				X [1]	X
Iron/manganese – insoluble						X				X
Nitrate				X	X [5]		X			
Odor and off-taste	X	X	X	X	X		X		X	
Some pesticides [6]	X [6]						X [6]			
Radium				X	X		X			
Radon gas	X	X								
Salt				X			X			
Sand, silt, clay (turbidity)						X				
Volatile organic chemicals	X	X		X [7]			X			
Water hardness					X					

[1] When followed by mechanical filtration or an activated carbon filter.

[2] Mercury only.

[3] Barium only.

[4] When present in low concentrations.

[5] Anion exchange units will remove nitrate. But cation exchange units will not.

[6] For information on ways to treat water for specific pesticides, obtain pesticide health advisory summaries (see pages 145-146).

[7] Works for volatile organic chemicals with high boiling points.

WATER-TREATMENT SCAMS

What to look for

Many water-treatment scams follow two patterns. Salespeople may try to sell devices that really don't work, or they may sell devices to consumers who really don't need them. To do this, many scam artists try the following strategies:

- They take advantage of fear and ignorance about water quality instead of relying on the quality and effectiveness of their product.
- They test water in the home, which may not be an accurate procedure.
- They pretend to be taking a survey, giving away prizes in a contest, or working for the government.
- They claim their product has been approved or recommended by the U.S. Environmental Protection Agency. However, the EPA does not test or approve water-treatment devices. It only registers them.
- They want you to make an on-the-spot decision, instead of giving you time to shop around and think about your purchase.

What to do

- Have water tested by a government agency or a private laboratory that does not sell home water-treatment devices. When you know what contaminants are in your water, carefully examine all water-treatment options.
- Rent a water-treatment system and evaluate its performance prior to purchase.
- Never give your credit card number over the phone unless you are familiar with the company.
- Read all contracts carefully.
- Call the Better Business Bureau or a consumer protection agency to find out if there are any unresolved complaints about the company.
- If you are the victim of scare tactics or misleading advertising, call or write to your Better Business Bureau, the Federal Trade Commission, the Cooperative Extension Service, the Water Quality Association, the state and U.S. EPA, local and state health departments, or local media.

WHAT ABOUT DEVICES THAT USE MAGNETIC FIELDS?

In the search for water-treatment devices, you may hear about equipment that uses magnetic fields, electrostatic fields, or other physical forces to treat water. Backers of these devices claim that the equipment will eliminate corrosion, scale, bacteria, algae, and other assorted problems. However, independent studies have found most of these devices to be ineffective and without scientific basis.

When confronted with a suspicious device, consult your local department of public health, Cooperative Extension Service, or the Better Business Bureau.

Miscellaneous

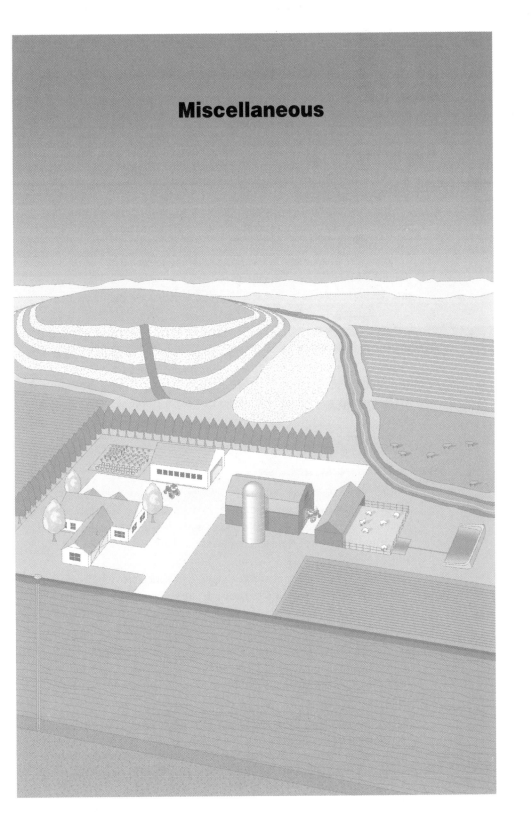

Store livestock waste wisely

Feedlot facts

It's not a pleasant statistic: A 100-cow dairy herd can produce as much waste as 2,400 people.

But that's not the only unpleasant fact: In certain types of soil, this waste can seep through the ground and reach groundwater, contaminating it with nitrate and bacteria.

In most cases, animal waste must be stored temporarily before it can be disposed of or used. The waste can either be stored for a few days on the feedlot, or it can be stored for several months or more in waste storage structures.

Storage on the feedlot

If you store animal waste on the feedlot, locate the lot far away and downhill from any wells, sinkholes, or surface water. Make provisions to collect runoff water from the feedlot for proper disposal. Also, remember to remove new waste deposits every few days. Wastes are usually spread as fertilizer.

Waste storage structures

Waste storage structures allow you the flexibility of determining the proper time to field-apply manure to use it as fertilizer. But just as with a feedlot, waste storage structures should not be located near surface water or wells. Check local and state requirements before beginning construction of a structure.

In many cases, unlined, earthen storage facilities provide livestock producers with a low-cost alternative to storing wastes in concrete or metal structures. The three most common earthen structures are earthen storage basins, anaerobic treatment lagoons, and runoff holding ponds.

Earthen storage basins. These are small, short-term storage ponds that hold concentrated manure until it can be hauled. They replace the concrete and steel storage tanks. However, these concentrated wastes can cause odor problems.

Anaerobic lagoons. These are manure-treatment facilities, which must be designed for the amount of manure they receive. A lagoon is considerably larger than an earthen storage basin. Also, the manure it holds is not as concentrated as that in an earthen basin. The manure is diluted with water and undergoes anaerobic decomposition. A lagoon must be pumped down once or twice each year, but it should not be emptied.

Runoff holding ponds. These are storage ponds that collect the runoff water coming from an uncovered feedlot. Before reaching the holding pond, the runoff water goes through a settling basin where the solids settle out. The holding pond should be regularly pumped empty on the land, as long as doing so will not create a pollution problem.

Divert extraneous water away from earthen structures. This can be done by installing gutters on roofs. Terraces around the earthen structure can divert surface water, preventing it from entering the basin, lagoon, or holding pond.

Seepage

With all earthen structures, the greatest groundwater concern is that wastes will seep through the bottom of the basin to groundwater. However, seepage is usually *not* a problem if the earthen structure has a clay bottom.

When the bottom of the structure is something other than clay—sandy soil, gravelly soil, or fractured rock, for instance—you must seal it. Sealing can be done with compacted clay, plastic lining, or any other material that keeps water from seeping through the ground.

Some states require that soil borings be made to determine the composition of the soil and evaluate the risk of seepage. Also, some states require that the earthen structure design be approved by a registered engineer or someone with equivalent credentials.

Vegetative filters

Infiltration areas, such as vegetative filters, are sometimes used as an alternative to runoff holding ponds. And like holding ponds, they must be preceded by a settling basin.

Vegetative filters channel runoff water from the feedlot, allowing it to be taken up by the vegetation. Runoff also infiltrates the soil, but it is believed that vegetative filters do not pose a groundwater hazard when they have been constructed properly.

Vegetative filters cannot handle large amounts of runoff water, so most states limit their use to small operations. In some states, "small" means operations with about 300 beef or dairy cattle or 750 hogs. Check with the state pollution control agency for guidelines because certain states do not permit the use of vegetative filters at all.

Solid-manure storage

Solid-manure storage is possible when you add enough bedding until the manure contains enough solids to be stacked in a pile. To prevent leaching to groundwater and to make loading easier, stack manure solids on a concrete pad.

Cover the storage area with a roof to prevent rain and snow from causing the manure to run off. This will not only prevent groundwater contamination but also will preserve the nutrient value of the manure.

Collect any runoff from the solid-manure storage area, and apply it to growing crops.

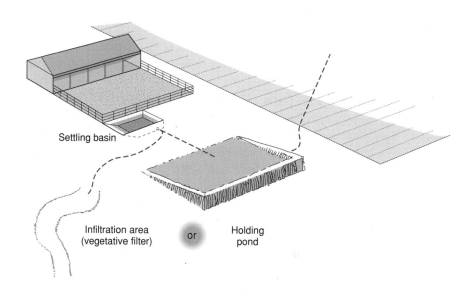

Settling basin

Infiltration area
(vegetative filter)

or

Holding
pond

Using compost piles for animal disposal

Mel Gerber recalls that he got "a lot of hoots in the coffee shop" when he first decided to try composting as a way to solve the common problem of dead pig disposal.

But now he is getting a lot of interest from both the University of Missouri and other farmers.

Renderers will not pick up animals in Morgan County, Missouri, where Gerber farms. So farmers have traditionally relied on burying or burning to dispose of dead pigs.

However, burning takes a lot of preparation and must be done in an approved incinerator to prevent air pollution. Burying takes time and effort, and concerns about groundwater contamination have led to restrictions on animal burial in many states, including the Show-Me State. So in 1990 Gerber became interested in a cheaper, safer, low-tech way to dispose of his animals.

Poultry producers across the country have had considerable success composting dead birds, but many people assumed composting wouldn't work for anything larger than turkeys. That may not necessarily be true. University research is just under way on the idea of composting larger animals, but Gerber's experience shows that the system has real potential.

Gerber uses large round bales to create three compost piles. The back wall of each compost pile consists of three bales, placed end to end. Each of the two side walls consists of two bales.

Every year, he adds 30 to 40 cubic yards of sawdust to the piles—sawdust obtained for free from a neighbor. Carcasses of the animals, some of them full-grown, mature sows, are completely buried in the sawdust.

The compost piles are placed away from streams and wells, and altogether they take up a space that is 40 feet long by 12 feet wide.

After two years of use, Gerber says animal disposal is easier than it has ever been, and major problems have not materialized.

"The soft tissue decomposes rapidly, leaving no hides," he says. "Amazingly, even the larger bones, such as jawbones, decompose a lot."

Gerber applies the compost material on a pasture twice a year, and he says you can still see some small bone fragments. "This might be a problem for some people, but after a week I can't see any bones." However, he says that when he makes hay on this pasture, he does encounter some small fragments.

The compost piles have not created problems with rats nor significant problems with dogs, Gerber also notes. What's more, odor has not been an issue, and he has had no complaints from neighbors.

"The only time you get a strong odor problem is briefly, when you stir the compost," he says.

Gerber's composting program is flexible, but the following schedule gives you a general idea of how it works:

- It takes three months to fill one compost bin.

- Six weeks after a bin is filled, he stirs the pile. He does this by using a front-end loader to move the pile to a new bin.

- Six weeks later he spreads the compost on his pasture.

- Whenever he stirs a pile during the winter, he adds about a quart of ammonium nitrate per pile to aid decomposition.

As for water quality, Gerber says he has not noticed any leachate coming from the compost piles. "If you use enough sawdust," he notes, "I don't think you'll have that problem."

"We're cautiously optimistic about this system of composting," says Charles Fulhage, an agricultural engineer with the University of Missouri.

Fulhage says composting larger animals may be most attractive to family farms. Large, commercial operations are more likely to be able to work out a contract with a rendering facility.

"So far, composting is superior to burying," Gerber notes. "It isn't even close."

47 Have old, underground fuel storage tanks removed

Leaking tanks

One out of every four regulated underground fuel tanks is leaking, according to the U.S. Environmental Protection Agency. And in some areas, the problem may be worse. For instance, the Illinois Office of the State Fire Marshal has found that 50 to 60 percent of the underground fuel storage tanks being removed have released some type of petroleum into the ground.

If these statistics don't catch your attention, here are a few more:

- Gasoline has been linked to certain forms of cancer.
- One gallon of gasoline can contaminate an estimated 750,000 gallons of water.
- Gasoline contains more than 200 different chemicals. One of those chemicals, benzene, has a federal drinking water standard of only 5 parts per billion (ppb), but humans can't detect it until levels reach 1,700 ppb.
- Nationally, underground tanks and pipes are estimated to be responsible for about 5 percent of all hazardous material spills.

Not only do leaking tanks threaten groundwater, but when petroleum gets into the soil, vapors can sometimes build up in confined spaces, such as septic tanks, sewers, and basements. This raises the risk of possible explosion.

Another reason for concern is that if the problem is allowed to get out of hand, the cost of cleanup can get out of hand as well. When farmers sell property that contains an underground tank, leaking or not, some realtors and lending institutions require them to verify the condition of the tank. Lending institutions may also raise the question of liability for future groundwater contamination.

All in all, there are strong incentives to remove underground tanks.

What causes leaks?

Tanks leak for many reasons. Piping may be improperly installed, the tank may be overfilled, or the tank walls may corrode. A 1989 study in Wisconsin found that out of 35,292 registered agricultural tanks, 30,132 were made of either bare steel or coated steel—material that is especially susceptible to corrosion. If an underground tank is more than 10 years old, and if it is made of bare steel or coated steel, the chances for a leak are increased dramatically, says the National Farm Medicine Center in Wisconsin.

Whether the source of trouble is corrosion or something else, it is important to remove leaking tanks or old underground tanks not in use.

How to locate a leak

To determine whether your underground storage tank is leaking, consider these questions from the National Farm Medicine Center. If the answer to one or more of the questions is yes, then you may have a leaking tank.

- Are you putting more fuel in than you are getting out? Monitor your gasoline input and output carefully.
- Is the soil near your underground tank saturated with petroleum?
- Is there a sheen of petroleum on the surface of nearby ponds and streams?
- Can you smell a strong petroleum odor coming from the soil or water around your underground tank or home?
- Do neighbors complain about a petroleum odor—in sewer lines, sumps, or basements, for example?
- Have you noticed a strange taste or smell to your water?
- Is your suction pump rattling, or does petroleum flow from it un- evenly?
- Does the pump hesitate more than usual before dispensing petroleum?
- Is there water in the tank of your car or tractor? It's normal to have a small amount of water in the tank due to condensation from the air. But if the amount of water increases over days and weeks, water could be seeping into the underground tank. If water can get *into* the tank, that means petroleum can leak *out*.

What happens when you find a leak?

If you find that your underground tank is leaking, check with the local emergency response agency and consider evacuating the area. "Do not smoke, and extinguish all open flames in the area," recommends the National Farm Medicine Center. "Do not use water. Turn off electrical equipment in the area. Any source of heat or sparks can cause an explo- sion. Call your local fire department, and ask officials to test for explo- sive conditions. They can also help you decide what to do next."

Also, when a leak is discovered, the soil will have to be tested for contamination. The procedure for taking a soil sample is extremely im- portant, so check with the state environmental agency for information.

How to locate an abandoned tank

In some cases, you may not even know if there is an underground tank on your property—a tank that was abandoned years go.

To find out if your property contains a tank, contact your local fire chief, the state Fire Marshal's office, former property owners, neighbors, or local companies that might have filled the tank when it was in use. Also, look for old vent or fill pipes, and check fire insurance plan drawings for any sign of underground tanks. Old photographs might show fuel pumps or buildings where a tank was located. Another idea is to search for the tank with a metal detector.

Tank removal, installation, repairs

If you want to remove, install, or repair an underground storage tank, check with the state Fire Marshal's office to find out what regulations govern these actions. Some states require that all installations, repairs, or removals be done by a contractor registered with the Fire Marshal's office.

The reason for such regulations is safety. As an example of the hazards involved: One man was killed in an explosion when he was cutting apart a fuel tank. Another man was killed when installing a tank because an excavation wall collapsed on him.

Alternatives

If you are thinking about installing an underground storage tank, seriously consider the alternatives: Contract with a local gas station, use an above-ground storage tank, or use liquid propane or natural gas for home heating.

Security

To prevent vandals from getting to an above-ground tank, construct a concrete pad with a security fence around it.

48 Dispose of other hazardous waste safely

Disposal guide

There's more to hazardous waste on the farm than pesticide and fertilizer. A typical farm includes many other forms of waste that pose hazards to your health and groundwater.

In particular, you probably produce hazardous waste when operating and maintaining your farming equipment. For example, a hazard can arise when you leave old equipment on your land so you can salvage parts from it. Quite often, the batteries and oil are left to rot in these abandoned vehicles. Lead-acid batteries can contain 18 pounds of toxic metals and 1 gallon of corrosive, lead-contaminated acids. If the equipment corrodes, these chemicals can contaminate soil and may find their way into your groundwater.

The three main categories of waste that you should be concerned about are farm-equipment fluids, batteries, and paints and solvents.

Farm-equipment fluids

Motor oil. An estimated 450 million gallons of used oil are improperly disposed of every year in the United States. Although most waste oil is produced by automobiles and industry, farmers still have reason to be concerned. A typical farmer buys an average of 50 gallons of motor oil each year.

Used oil should never be mixed with *any* farm chemicals under any circumstances. Your best option is to recycle your oil. Contact common recycling sites such as local oil distributors, auto-repair stations, and commercial recycling services, or call the Cooperative Extension Service to find recyclers in your area. When storing oil before recycling, be sure it is in a sealed container such as a steel drum or plastic jug. Make sure the container is clean.

Some states allow you to burn used oil in a used-oil fired space heater—but only under certain conditions. Check with the state's major environmental agency to find out when this is allowed.

Antifreeze. Antifreeze can be very dangerous because its sweet taste attracts animals. Five tablespoons of antifreeze can kill a 25-pound dog.

Your first step should be to find out if the store that sells the antifreeze will take back the used product. Your next option is to contact a commercial recycling operation. If that doesn't work, try your local wastewater treatment plant. Some wastewater treatment and disposal plants that used to accept antifreeze don't accept it any longer. So check with your local plant to make sure.

Fuels. Uncontaminated gasoline can be used up in engines. But if the gasoline is contaminated, contact the Cooperative Extension Service or hazardous waste agency to determine a proper disposal method.

Gasoline can become contaminated when used as a solvent for cleaning tools. To avoid this problem, as well as the hazards posed by gasoline, you should clean tools with commercially available solvents, such as mineral spirits. These products can often be mixed with motor oil and then recycled. (Check with your recycling center first.)

Also, do not leave fuel stored in small containers for a long time, such as over the winter. The fuel decays over time.

Batteries

As mentioned earlier, old batteries should not be abandoned and left to corrode. Also, do not dispose of lead-acid batteries at a landfill; this is illegal in some states.

Instead, batteries can be recycled, repaired, and reused. You should be able to trade in your old battery at the store where you bought it or at the store where you are purchasing your new battery. Otherwise, you may be able to have batteries recycled at such places as service stations, auto parts stores, auto parts warehouses, discount stores, and junkyards. Contact your Extension office for recycling locations.

Household batteries can also contribute to pollution if they are casually discarded. In particular, small batteries like the ones used in calculators, pagers, cameras, and watches often contain mercury, an extremely dangerous heavy metal. Experimental recycling programs for these batteries are being tried in several states, so keep your eyes open for these programs.

Cleaners, solvents, and paints

Cleaners and solvents. Seal used cleaners and solvents in a jar until the particles settle out. Then strain the substance left in the bottom of the jar. That way, you can reuse the cleaner or solvent. Wrap the waste solids in several layers of newspaper and dispose of them in a landfill.

Paints. It is ideal if you can use up paint in a manner consistent with label instructions. But if that is not possible, and if there are no hazardous waste collections in your area, your last resort is evaporation. Evaporate water- and oil-based paints in a secure, outdoor area away from flames, children, and animals. Paints can also be solidified using sand, sawdust, kitty litter, or dirt as an absorbent material. Take the solid residue and dispose of it in a landfill.

Wood preservatives. Do not solidify, burn, or bury leftover wood preservative. Also, never burn any wood that has been treated with wood preservative. The best option is to keep wood preservatives in a secure container and wait until a household hazardous waste collection day is held in your area.

Guidelines

There are too many chemicals, compounds, and substances in a home or on a farm to be listed in this book, but here are some general guidelines when using any product.

- Always read the label and follow all usage and disposal instructions.
- Buy only the amount you need.
- Try to use up the leftover portion, but only if necessary.
- If you have some leftover product, give it to neighbors, friends, or community groups who need it—but only if the product is in its original container.
- Store drums that contain hazardous waste on pallets—over a solid floor, if possible. This will make it easier to spot leaks and will discourage rust and corrosion.
- Never bury waste or dump waste in a ditch or field. You also shouldn't burn waste, although sometimes the product label allows this under certain conditions.
- Find out whether your community has hazardous waste collection days. If it doesn't, talk to neighbors about proposing a collection program.
- For information on how to start a recycling or collection program, contact the nearest Cooperative Extension Service office.

49 Take precautions when irrigating

A good thing, but...

Water can be too much of a good thing when you irrigate, from both a crop production and a water quality standpoint. Too much water can lead to increased leaching of nitrate and pesticides. It can carry some nitrate and pesticides from the target area to groundwater.

There are three main types of irrigation, and each has its own special benefits and problems when it comes to groundwater.

Flood or furrow irrigation

With flood irrigation, water is pumped or allowed to flow into a ridged or diked area of the field. With furrow irrigation, water is ponded between crop rows created during planting and cultivation.

The basic risk with these systems is overapplication of water. Overapplication increases the chances that surface-applied or soil-incorporated pesticides will leach to the groundwater supply—particularly if the soil is highly permeable. Because it is harder to control irrigation water with flood and furrow systems, it is important to use flow meters, surge valves, and reuse basins. Flow meters allow you to measure the amount of water being applied, surge valves make sure water flows evenly, and reuse basins catch water at the ends of rows, then return it to the system.

Sprinkler irrigation

Sprinkler irrigation sprays water into the air through perforated pipes or nozzles. For row crops, this system poses the least risk to groundwater because water can be applied more precisely than with flood or furrow irrigation.

Also, a sprinkler irrigation system makes it easier to put down nitrogen in split applications. With split applications, less N is lost, reducing the risk to groundwater.

Trickle or drip irrigation

This irrigation method applies water very slowly on or beneath the soil surface near the plant. Because this method doesn't use much water, it is probably the safest in terms of leaching. However, trickle irrigation is not practical for row crops. There is also the potential for over-application, as with all other systems. Overapplication could mean increased leaching.

How to time irrigation

If possible, delay irrigation for at least one day after applying a chemical. This will give the chemical a chance to degrade and attach to soil particles. If the chemical is postemergent, delaying irrigation will also give the chemical a chance to be taken up by the plant.

Note: If there has been more than 1 inch of rain or irrigation water on the land in the past twenty-four hours, the ground is probably too wet to apply chemicals without excessive leaching.

Testing irrigation water

In the arid regions of the Midwest, there is more risk of nitrate buildup in water than in the wetter regions. Therefore, it is important in dry regions to test irrigation water to find out how much nitrogen it contains. In some cases, irrigation water can contribute from 50 to 100 pounds of nitrogen per acre.

Pesticide leaching

As you can see, the potential for irrigation to increase leaching depends on several factors, such as the type of irrigation system, soil, and pesticide. The following chart, developed by the U.S. Environmental Protection Agency, shows how these factors affect the possibility of pesticide leaching.

Irrigation potential for pesticide leaching

	Sprinkler			Drip			Flood		
	Clay	Loam	Sand	Clay	Loam	Sand	Clay	Loam	Sand
Foliar-applied	L	M	M	L	L	L	L	L	L
Surface-applied									
Preplant/preemergent	L	M	M	L	L	M	M	M	H
Postemergent	L	M	M	L	L	M	M	M	M
Soil-incorporated									
Preplant/preemergent	M	M	H	L	M	M	M	H	H
Postemergent	L	M	H	L	M	M	M	M	H

Irrigation method and soil type

NOTE: L = Low leaching potential
          M = Moderate leaching potential
          H = High leaching potential

This table assumes that the pesticide being used is one that will leach, given the opportunity. Actual leaching potential will depend on the specific pesticide and site properties.

SOURCE: *Protecting Ground Water: Pesticides and Agricultural Practices*, U.S. Environmental Protection Agency, 1988.

Cutting back on nitrogen and irrigating efficiently

Milton Ruhter has been farming for 48 years, but he says he's not too old to learn something new.

For the past two years, Ruhter has been a cooperator in the Mid-Nebraska Water Quality Demonstration Project, which focuses on irrigation, nitrogen, and pesticide management. One of the lessons he and many other cooperators have learned is that going above the recommended rates for nitrogen isn't worth the extra cost.

In the test plots on his farm, Ruhter applied nitrogen at the recommended rate, 50 pounds per acre *above* the recommended rate, and 50 pounds per acre *below* the recommended rate. The yield differences among all three rates were so negligible that the lowest rate came out as the best choice economically—at least for the two years that Ruhter has been part of the program.

Agronomists caution, however, that it is unknown whether applying below recommended rates for an extended time will work. But the point remains that applying nitrogen *above* the recommended level does not pay off.

To avoid excessive rates, soil testing and crediting nitrogen are critical. On Ruhter's test plots, agronomists sample the soil down to 4 feet, so Ruhter knows the level of residual nitrogen in the soil. Ruhter also credits nitrogen provided by the previous year's soybean crop and tests his irrigation water for nitrogen levels.

With all of this information, he has an accurate handle on how much nitrogen is already there and how much must be applied to meet the yield goal.

Another way Ruhter increases the efficiency of his nitrogen program is by applying 28 percent in split applications. As part of his ridge-tillage system, he bands nitrogen at planting and again at cultivation and hilling. By spoon-feeding nitrogen to his crop at different times, he says there is less risk that a single rainfall will cause it to be lost through leaching.

To manage irrigation more efficiently, agronomists use moisture blocks to measure soil moisture on Ruhter's plots. The agronomists monitor moisture blocks once a week at 1-, 2-, and 3-foot levels. They also use an atmometer to estimate the amount of moisture being taken up by the crop.

With information on soil moisture and the amount of moisture being used by the crop, Ruhter knows how much irrigation water is required.

"A lot of people overirrigate because they think the topsoil has to stay wet all of the time," Ruhter says. "But you don't know for sure whether you need to irrigate unless you check moisture in the soil profile."

Ruhter has also started using surge valves, which more efficiently move the water in his furrow irrigation system. Without surge valves, you have to apply much more water to reach the lower end of the field, he notes. Excess water moving into the soil means excess leaching, more nutrient loss, more pesticide loss, and more risk of groundwater contamination.

In addition to irrigation and nitrogen management, Ruhter has been trying to cut back on pesticide rates by scouting and by relying on corn borer-resistant hybrids.

"We've definitely seen a difference," he says. "We had one year in which corn borers cut off the tops of most of the stalks of one hybrid, but the stalks of the resistant hybrid remained intact.

"Profits are thin, so farmers think before they spend any more money," Ruhter adds. "It makes us good operators."

50 Take precautions when chemigating

Pros and cons

Chemigation, the application of agrichemicals through an irrigation system, has some advantages over other application techniques:

- It applies pesticides more uniformly.
- It reduces mechanical damage to crops.
- It reduces hazards to the operator.

However, you need to supervise a chemigation system carefully to prevent overwatering with the water-chemical mixture.

Safety requirements

When you chemigate, install and properly maintain protective devices. Without these devices, a system failure could cause the chemicals to flow back directly into your well.

The requirements for chemigation antipollution devices vary from state to state. But to get the most protection, consider the safeguards depicted in the illustration on page 179. Also, contact your Cooperative Extension Service office to find out about your state's regulations on chemigation.

Other points

- Check your unattended chemigation system frequently.
- Always use the least amount of water possible. Use only enough water to transport and activate the chemical.
- Don't apply a chemical through a chemigation system unless the container label says it is all right.
- Don't chemigate with a sprinkler system if wind speeds are greater than 5 miles per hour; otherwise, the chemical could drift.
- Don't connect your irrigation system directly to a public water supply when using chemigation. This is illegal in most states. Instead, collect the public water in a reservoir tank that has a fixed air gap between the pipe inlet and the water source. Pump water from this reservoir.
- Don't inject an agrichemical into your irrigation system on the suction side of the irrigation pump. This is illegal. It defeats the purpose of the system's safety devices.

Pesticide leaching

To find out how different soil types affect the risk of pesticide leaching with chemigation, check the following chart from the U.S. Environmental Protection Agency.

Chemigation potential for pesticide leaching

Chemigation method and soil type								
Sprinkler			Drip			Flood		
Clay	Loam	Sand	Clay	Loam	Sand	Clay	Loam	Sand
L	M	H	L	M	M	M	H	H

NOTE: L = Low leaching potential
M = Moderate leaching potential
H = High leaching potential

This table assumes that the pesticide being used is one that will leach, given the opportunity. Actual leaching potential will depend on the specific pesticide and site properties.

SOURCE: *Protecting Ground Water: Pesticides and Agricultural Practices*, U.S. Environmental Protection Agency, 1988.

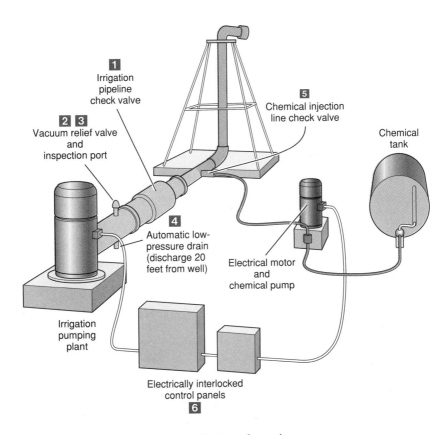

1 Irrigation
pipeline
check valve

2 3
Vacuum relief valve
and
inspection port

5
Chemical injection
line check valve

Chemical
tank

4 Automatic low-
pressure drain
(discharge 20
feet from well)

Electrical motor
and
chemical pump

Irrigation
pumping
plant

Electrically interlocked
control panels
6

Antipollution safeguards

To offer the most protection against well contamination, your chemigation system
should have these safeguards:

1. **The irrigation pipeline check valve** prevents the chemical and water mixture from
   backflowing into the well. Some states require this to be a double check valve,
   whereas others only require a single check valve.

2. **The vacuum relief valve** on the irrigation pipeline also prevents the backflow of
   chemical solution.

3. **The inspection port** is used to check how the valves are working.

4. **The automatic low-pressure drain** is used to drain the chemical and water mixture
   left in the lines when the system is turned off. The drain should discharge the chemical and water mixture at least 20 feet from any water supply.

5. **The chemical injection line check valve** prevents the flow of fluid back toward the
   injection pump.

6. **Electronically interlocked control panels** will stop the chemical from pumping whenever the water pump stops.

For More Information

Regional offices
U.S. Environmental Protection Agency

Groundwater and drinking water branch chiefs

Regional groundwater and drinking water branch chiefs can supply you with information on EPA regulations and programs. Drinking water chiefs can supply information about public water supplies and drinking water standards, whereas groundwater chiefs can field questions about groundwater safety and well testing. Groundwater chiefs can also provide information about wellhead protection programs.

	Groundwater	Drinking water
REGION 1 Boston, MA	(617)565-3610	(617)565-3610
REGION 2 New York, NY	(212)264-1800	(212)264-1800
REGION 3 Philadelphia, PA	(215)597-8826	(215)597-8826
REGION 4 Atlanta, GA	(404)347-3379	(404)347-2207
REGION 5 Chicago, IL	(312)886-1490	(312)353-2151
REGION 6 Dallas, TX	(214)655-6446	(214)655-7150
REGION 7 Kansas City, KS	(913)551-7033	(913)551-7032
REGION 8 Denver, CO	(303)294-1135	(303)293-1413
REGION 9 San Francisco, CA	(415)744-1817	(415)744-1817
REGION 10 Seattle, WA	(206)553-4092	(206)553-4092

Regional Offices of Underground Storage Tanks

U.S. EPA Regional Offices of Underground Storage Tanks can provide you with federal technical standards for storage tanks. To find out more about specific regulations and standards for underground storage tanks in your state, call your state's program (see pages 186-187).

REGION 1
Boston, MA
(617)573-9604

REGION 2
New York, NY
(212)264-3384

REGION 3
Philadelphia, PA
(215)597-7354

REGION 4
Atlanta, GA
(404)347-3866

REGION 5
Chicago, IL
(312)886-6159

REGION 6
Dallas, TX
(214)655-6755

REGION 7
Kansas City, KS
(913)551-7055

REGION 8
Denver, CO
(303)293-1514

REGION 9
San Francisco, CA
(415)744-2079

REGION 10
Seattle, WA
(206)553-1643

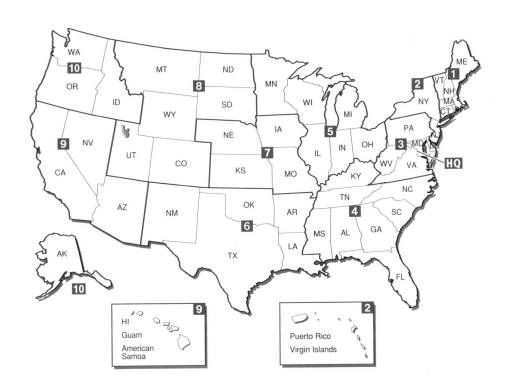

National Pesticide Telecommunications Network

Phone: (800)858-7378

Fax: (806)743-3094

Hours: 24 hours a day, every day of the year

Services:

- Information on the recognition and management of pesticide poisonings.
- Referrals for laboratory analysis, investigation of pesticide incidents, and emergency treatment information.
- Information on safety, environmental and health effects, and cleanup and disposal procedures.

Safe Drinking Water Hotline

Phone: (800)426-4791

Hours: Monday through Friday, 8 a.m. to 4:30 p.m., Central Standard Time

Services:

- Information on all hazardous chemicals, including possible health effects and contamination sources.
- Referrals for water-testing laboratories in your area.
- Information such as: what to look for and test for in private and public wells, how to construct wells, and how to store and handle chemicals.
- Explanation and clarification of the Safe Drinking Water Act.

State offices

State drinking water agencies

Every state in the United States has a drinking water agency that can answer questions about drinking water regulations and programs in its state.

ALABAMA
Montgomery
(205)271-7773

ALASKA
Juneau
(907)465-5314

ARIZONA
Phoenix
(602)207-4617

ARKANSAS
Little Rock
(501)661-2623

CALIFORNIA
Sacramento
(916)323-1382

COLORADO
Denver
(303)692-3546

CONNECTICUT
Hartford
(203)566-1251

DELAWARE
Dover
(302)739-5410

FLORIDA
Tallahassee
(904)487-1762

GEORGIA
Atlanta
(404)656-5660

HAWAII
Honolulu
(808)586-4258

IDAHO
Boise
(208)334-5860

ILLINOIS
Springfield
(217)785-8653

INDIANA
Indianapolis
(317)233-4222

IOWA
Des Moines
(515)281-8869

KANSAS
Topeka
(913)296-5503

KENTUCKY
Frankfort
(502)564-3410

LOUISIANA
New Orleans
(504)568-5105

MAINE
Augusta
(207)289-2070

MARYLAND
Dundalk
(410)631-3702

MASSACHUSETTS
Boston
(617)292-5529

MICHIGAN
Lansing
(517)335-8326

MINNESOTA
Minneapolis
(612)627-5133

MISSISSIPPI
Jackson
(601)960-7518

MISSOURI
Jefferson City
(314)751-5331

MONTANA
Helena
(406)444-2406

NEBRASKA
Lincoln
(402)471-2541

NEVADA
Carson City
(702)687-6615

NEW HAMPSHIRE
Concord
(603)271-3139

NEW JERSEY
Trenton
(609)292-5550

NEW MEXICO
Santa Fe
(505)827-2778

NEW YORK
Albany
(518)458-6731

NORTH CAROLINA
Raleigh
(919)733-2321

NORTH DAKOTA
Bismarck
(701)221-5225

SOUTH CAROLINA
Columbia
(803)734-5310

VIRGINIA
Richmond
(804)786-5566

OHIO
Columbus
(614)644-2752

SOUTH DAKOTA
Pierre
(605)773-3754

WASHINGTON
Olympia
(206)753-3466

OKLAHOMA
Oklahoma City
(405)271-5205

TENNESSEE
Nashville
(615)532-0191

WASHINGTON, D.C.
Washington, D.C.
(202)404-1120

OREGON
Portland
(503)731-4010

TEXAS
Austin
(512)908-6930

WEST VIRGINIA
Charleston
(304)558-2981

PENNSYLVANIA
Harrisburg
(717)787-9037

UTAH
Salt Lake City
(801)538-6159

WISCONSIN
Madison
(608)267-7651

RHODE ISLAND
Providence
(401)277-6867

VERMONT
Waterbury
(802)244-1562

WYOMING
Cheyenne
(307)777-7781

State underground storage tank programs

State underground storage tank program offices can provide specific information about regulations and programs in their state. Note that some offices have separate numbers for information about leaking tanks.

ALABAMA
Montgomery
(205)271-7986
For leaking tank information, call (205)270-5655.

ALASKA
Juneau
(907)465-5200

ARIZONA
Phoenix
(602)207-4261

ARKANSAS
Little Rock
(501)562-6533

CALIFORNIA
Sacramento
(916)227-4400

COLORADO
Denver
(303)289-5643
For leaking tank information, call (303)692-3330.

CONNECTICUT
Hartford
(203)566-4630
For leaking tank information, call (203)566-4633.

DELAWARE
New Castle
(302)323-4588

FLORIDA
Tallahassee
(904)488-3935

GEORGIA
Atlanta
(404)362-2687

HAWAII
Honolulu
(808)586-4228

IDAHO
Boise
(208)334-5860

ILLINOIS
Springfield
(217)785-5878
For leaking tank information, call (217)782-6761. To report a leaking tank, call (800)782-7860.

INDIANA
Indianapolis
(317)233-3560

IOWA
Des Moines
(515)281-8135

KANSAS
Topeka
(913)296-1685
For leaking tank informa-
tion, call (913)296-4367.

KENTUCKY
Frankfort
(502)564-6716

LOUISIANA
Baton Rouge
(504)765-0243

MAINE
Augusta
(207)287-2651

MARYLAND
Baltimore
(410)631-3442

MASSACHUSETTS
Tewksbury
(508)851-9813
For leaking tank informa-
tion, call Boston:
(617)556-1044.

MICHIGAN
Lansing
(517)322-1935
For leaking tank informa-
tion, call (517)373-8168.

MINNESOTA
St. Paul
(612)297-8679
For leaking tank informa-
tion, call (612)297-8574.
To report a leaking tank,
call (612)649-5451 or
(800)422-0798.

MISSISSIPPI
Jackson
(601)961-5171

MISSOURI
Jefferson City
(314)751-6822

MONTANA
Helena
(406)444-5970

NEBRASKA
Lincoln
(402)471-9465

NEVADA
Carson City
(702)687-5872

NEW HAMPSHIRE
Concord
(603)271-3644

NEW JERSEY
Trenton
(609)984-3156

NEW MEXICO
Santa Fe
(505)827-0188

NEW YORK
Albany
(518)457-4351

NORTH CAROLINA
Raleigh
(919)733-8486

NORTH DAKOTA
Bismarck
(701)221-5166
To report a leaking tank,
call (800)472-2121.

OHIO
Reynoldsburg
(614)752-7938

OKLAHOMA
Oklahoma City
(405)521-3107
For leaking tank informa-
tion, call (405)521-6575.

OREGON
Portland
(503)229-5733
For leaking tank informa-
tion, call (503)229-6170.

PENNSYLVANIA
Harrisburg
(717)772-5599

RHODE ISLAND
Providence
(401)277-2234

SOUTH CAROLINA
Columbia
(803)734-5331

SOUTH DAKOTA
Pierre
(605)773-3296

TENNESSEE
Nashville
(615)532-0945

TEXAS
Austin
(512)908-2200

UTAH
Salt Lake City
(801)536-4100

VERMONT
Waterbury
(802)244-8702

VIRGINIA
Richmond
(804)527-5192

WASHINGTON
Olympia
(206)459-6272

WASHINGTON, D.C.
Washington, D.C.
(202)404-1167

WEST VIRGINIA
Charleston
(304)558-6371

WISCONSIN
Madison
(608)267-1384
For leaking tank informa-
tion, call (608)267-7560.

WYOMING
Cheyenne
(307)777-7781

Rinse pad designs

For more detailed information about rinse pad designs, contact the following sources. If you cannot reach any of the following sources, try contacting your area Extension agent or local land-grant university.

MidWest Plan Service
122 Davidson Hall
Iowa State University
Ames, IA 50011-3080
(515)294-4337

David Kammel
University of Wisconsin
Agricultural Engineering
    Department
460 Henry Mall
Madison, WI 53706
(608)262-9776

National Agricultural Chemicals
    Association
1155 15th St. NW
Suite 900
Washington, DC 20005
(202)296-1585

Agricultural Retailers Association
339 Consort Drive
Manchester, MO 63011
(314)256-4900

Field Crop Scouting Manual

The *Field Crop Scouting Manual*, a 146-page book, describes detailed scouting procedures and includes full-color photos of common crop insects, weeds, and diseases.

You can obtain a copy for $20 by writing to the Vocational Agriculture Service, College of Agriculture, University of Illinois, 1401 S. Maryland Drive, Urbana, IL 61801; or call (217)333-3871. Make checks payable to the University of Illinois.

Also, be sure to add the following shipping and handling costs:

For orders under $25 .... add $3

For orders from $25 to $100 .... add 8 percent

For orders from $100.01 to $500 .... add 7 percent

For orders over $500 .... add 6 percent

The University of Illinois Plant Clinic

The University of Illinois Plant Clinic diagnoses plant samples for insect, weed, and disease problems. This service, available between May and September, is offered for a nominal fee. To submit a sample, follow these steps:

1. Send in as much of the plant as possible—roots, stem, and leaves.
2. Keep the roots, with soil attached, enclosed in a plastic bag.
3. Seal the plastic bag at the soil line so the top of the plant is sticking out of the bag.
4. Wrap everything in newspaper and place it in a box.
5. Enclose as much background information as possible about the problem, symptoms, and cultural practices. You can obtain a field history from your local Cooperative Extension Service office.
6. Mail the plant sample to: Plant Clinic, 1401 W. St. Mary's Road, Urbana, IL 61801. *Do not* put "University of Illinois" on the envelope.

information services

Information Services provides communications support for the Cooperative Extension Service, Agricultural Experiment Station, and other groups within the College of Agriculture, University of Illinois at Urbana-Champaign. Services include publication and videotape production, photography, printing and distribution, teleconferencing, and news reports for print and broadcast media.

For more information on our services or to obtain a free copy of a *Resources Catalog*, write or call:

University of Illinois
Office of Agricultural Communications and Education
Information Services
69-DP Mumford Hall
1301 West Gregory Drive
Urbana, IL 61801

(217)333-4780